Sunflowers
at the
End
of
Time

Tom Lewin

WORLDS
WITHIN

Published by:
Worlds Within
an imprint of White Rabbit House LLC
118e East 60th Street
New York, NY, 10022

ISBN: 979-8-218-54675-5
First Edition

Cover design and illustrations by Maia Benaim

*

Through swaying palms
I first saw those eyes

Sparkling lapis lazuli
jasmine scents
on that sand-swept
desert plain

Two caravans
heading for Mecca

Home passing me
in a flash of silk
under the stars

What countless
Mothers
those eyes
have hidden within!

*

Contents

*

Proof

Proof!

You ask for proof
lying here
drunk on the newness
of our bodies
in the espresso-soaked
morning sun
intertwined shyly
between my new bedsheets
in primordial fragrances
and last night's desire

Proof!
As if it were a formula
I could produce
from within my jacket pocket
thrown hastily on the floor
as we gave our gifts
while the rest of the world
was sleeping

Proof!
As if God
came with an instruction manual
like an Ikea flatpack
understood by some
and despised
by many

As though
the proof wasn't self-evident
in the birdsong in the street
or the fact
that they somehow returned
to the very same nest
without satellites or cartographers

As though
it wasn't right in front of us
as I ran my fingers across
the small of your naked back
breathing in your smile
and kissing your neck
that couldn't possibly be anything
but the masterwork of an Intelligence
transcending comprehension
The manic sculpting
of a brilliant and intuitive Creator

Footprints
of a Love so deep
we only sense
the *manifestations*
not the Architect

Searching
for the cathedral drawings
but only discovering
they'd been burned
in the night

You want proof
yet how can I explain
the familiarity of your face
topography
in those dark eyes
or the feeling
that I've been a young man before
many times over
and each time
fell madly
wildly in love
with the Feminine principle
and the smell of waking
with my nose pressed
between a woman's shoulders

You ask for proof
yet the more I open these eyes
the more I comprehend
that potent Truth
physicists stumbled across
arriving back
into the prehistoric hands
of songs
echoed in the *Vedas*

Proof
that Life's *living*
and God's a *word*
One that can never be understood
simply *pointed to*

In the same way
we can't prove our love
through anything but our actions
or amusement by laughing

And it's the *not knowing*
whether we'll make love again
making this moment
so hauntingly special

The fleeting montage of Life
that makes it livable

Proof's for the dead my dear
and let the dead have it!

For those of us
out here living
let us have *Mystery*
Chaos
that splash of uncertainty
imbuing every morning like this
with its Magic
every sorrow
with its poignance
and all moments
with their *sanctity*

Because I promise you
if proof truly was out there
in any tangible form

if I could leave you
this instant
and return in an hour
with a box
containing your desire
you'd no sooner
have opened it
than be searching
for a way
to *prove* its contents

See what's happening here?

What you want
is inseparable
from the question
and the words
leaving your lips
that so beautifully
whispered them
into my ear

Life is proof

We've Forgotten

We are
on the surface
flesh and bone

Nothing more
than a cluster
of organic matter
Existing in a Time
continuum

An endless cycle
of Birth and Death
at every second

At least
  that's what
    science
  would
    have
      you
        believe

Yet
how can science
that *altar* of rationality
have sent human beings
to the Moon
and remain cluelessly quagmired
in the origins of Consciousness?

Perhaps
it's because
we're probing
into a Phenomenon
repulsed
by measurements
dissections
and neat little
footnoted charts

We are looking in the wrong places

Somewhere
in our infatuation
with the Scientific Method
we've forgotten
we're more than our bodies

How can materialism
ever discover the origins
of creativity
joy
Love?

It's ludicrous

We've betrayed ourselves
Given our power away
to unconscious
egomaniacs
in high places

Terrified souls
who see Life
as nothing
but a clutching
for *more*

Yet
under a microscope
our cells are indistinguishable
from the Universe

This should be
the first clue

We're inseparable
from the natural environment
we dogmatically
pursue dominion over

The Divine Intelligence
maintaining the galaxial geometry
the billions of bodily processes
every second
is our *True Essence*

We seek external identities
and confusedly languish
forgetting
we're trying
to quantify
the Immeasurable

And yet
if we can sit
in the center
of our joy
our suffering
our fear
we'll discover
a stillness
defying description

It's the serenity
of the rising Sun
emerging
over an unspoiled
mountain valley

Let's discuss
our *truth*
here

Tell me
who you *are*
here

Words will be useless

A Collective Memory

There's a collective memory
on this planet
forgotten
in the archaic recesses
of our story

A resonance
deeper than culture
religious doctrine
social convention
or the petty and transient
isms
pegged to experience
since the birth
of civilization

Since our Ancestors
began weaving
this historical hallucination

It's the memory
of Nature
Cycles of Being

Before the oracles
and warlords
domestication of plants
institutions and slaughterhouses
before the beautification of saints

Before human beings
were *told*
who to deify
and procreate with

An echo
of a deeper connection
to the Cosmos
the Earth
Time's ebbing whirlpool
and the monumentality
of the Life journey

Yet
somewhere in history
we muffled memory
with verbosity
grandiosity
our collectively vacuous
self-importance

The shit-talking
of a million
arrogant empires
agencies
and banking cartels

We've forgotten
the subtle
sondic
reverberations

of an infinity
of loves
lives
memories
Beings
who've traversed
Saṃsāra

Don't Fall Asleep!

There's a message here
A *whisper*
in the silence
between moments

The *Unseen's* calling
longing
to
meet
you

Don't fall asleep!
Abandoning yourself
in endless distractions

The power mongers
need you *soft* and *sleepy*

Don't permit yourself to close over

Once closed
it's difficult to open
Because the bolts on the doors
multiply with the years

Speak less
Listen more
Avoid drowning
in *truths*

What is This Dance?

And what is this Dance
we're a part of?

This living
breathing
undulating
Phenomenon

What is this Magic
birthing Universes?

This Matrixial Mother
of all experience?

This *Shivic*
Creator and Destroyer
of worlds?

Do you
really think
we can catch it
name it
quantify it
understand it
like children
trying
to imprison
a beetle
in a matchbox?

How can we be
certain
we know more
about the Mystery
than those before us?

We namers of names
purveyors of semantics
builders of tall objects

We who can penetrate
the atomic fabric
and transmit thought
through the ether

Surely
our hubristic fantasy's
become *Olympian?*

Yet
one *honest* moment
in the presence
of unfiltered Reality
one unencumbered moment
engulfed by Nature's majesty
throws even Time and causality
onto shaky ground

Tongue-tied
by the terrifying buzz
beyond language

How can we
be certain
about Existence
when even physicists
are knocking
on *quantum* doors
that the mystical answers?

When
the observer
affects
the observed?

Claiming *Truth*
when we inhabit
undefinable worlds
each night!

Re-born
each morning
to a world
humming
with *Magick*

When plant matter
reveals the Heavens and *Hell*s
of our psyches
and human Life
emerges from a woman's Womb
and returns
to the Earth's

When
black holes
swallow
Light
Gravity
Time Itself
in a *logarithmic helix*

Even
at its most banal
we live and die
on a floating sphere
                    spirally
                speeding
                        through
                    space

And
you *know*
what This Is?

Art as Nourishment

For most people
art's an amenity

Puppetry
on the periphery
of Life

We consume
excrete
work
make love
sleep
and typically
art fills the blank spaces

The dull moments

Art's relegated
to entertainment

A medium
for mental dissolution
into Timelessness

A momentary abater
of obligations

Until the *wind changes*

We experience heartbreak
sudden illness
the Death of a loved one
Previously *unimaginable suffering*

Then something *curious* happens

Amid our anguish
we intuitively seek art
to understand
our agonizing human predicament

Art becomes a *meditation*

A conduit
for expressing
an inexpressible profundity
mocking logic

Suddenly
art becomes a crutch
a Life rope

And it begins to make sense
this miracle
humans instinctively receive
out of the metaphysical

This useless *hierophany*
shaking the core of our Being
emerges as a yearning *duende*

We begin to sense
art connects us
to those bewitched and bewildered
by the paradoxical weight
of *living*

Conversely
when our lives
are perforated
by unexpected elation
we seek art
to understand ourselves
and our experiences

In the throngs
of budding euphoria
we hunger to know
if anyone ever felt
this connected
to the synchronicities
of Life

Art becomes
a vital thread
reuniting us
with the immensity
of the human experience

The aeonic need
to express
our chrysalis of Reality

The craving
to be understood
and derive strength
from meaning
in our lives

Somehow
through the harmony
of sound and silence
light and shade
and form and space
we're *healed*

We're reminded of the Mystery

In the poignant moments
art's no longer
an indulgence
it's *nourishment*

The Past

Unfetter the past

Looking carefully
you'll notice
even *grief's* carried
into the eternal river
of moments

And all your lamenting
over losses
is in vain
if it doesn't teach you
that everything we lose
returns to us
in another form

Eventually
even sadness
looking back
becomes sweet
as your experiences
are washed away
by an invisible card dealer
who's trying to *reveal*
through each hand
how to let go and lean in
to this Mysterious Current
we strive and hanker
to spot our reflections in

like young lovers
discovering
their sweetheart's face
in the passing clouds

Those Windows to the Soul

How many sins
hide behind
these poker faces
gliding by
in these
serendipitous streets?

How bleak are the sorrows?

And what joys
unknowingly await
as the days evaporate
in a fever of emails
and shopping lists?

How many dreams
die under the glare
of watchful well-wishers?

And where do they go
resentfully forced to flee
nameless
in the dead of night
through back doors
and silent paddocks?

What perversions
do the mornings
gratefully wash away?

Regrets
does Time
thankfully soften?

And what becomes of their echoes
the memories
in the eyes of these souls
standing at traffic lights
and hurriedly passing me
in train stations?

Because
there's a tenderness
behind some eyes
briefly meeting mine

A brokenness
humanness
in these windows
that've absorbed
perhaps more
than they deserved to

Yet in others shrinks a fear
masked by pride and arrogance
Ignorance of the inherent Chaos
engulfing *all* living creatures

A refusal to surrender
to the fallibility
defining our experience here

Forgetting
each of us
walking these
temporary streets
want Life
Love
happiness
for ourselves
and our children

Neglecting the Truth
that all these eyes
no matter how far
they've strayed
from that inner *Eden*
need food
shelter
the chance to dream
and the comfort
in knowing
they've given their gifts
willingly

The assurance
that this peculiar moment
this *liminal flicker*
in Oblivion's cryptic vigil
has been lived
such that it
deepens
the Mystery

Our Hubris

We know *nothing*

Life's most uncomfortable
realization

And *truths* evaporate
behind the inexplicable threshold
of language's veil

For
all attempts
at understanding Reality
are but desperate groping's
for a Phenomenon
surpassing the linguistic domain
forming this phantasm

It's an unpopular opinion
understandably
as it births the potential
that all our endeavors
from *Vedanta*
and Bagdad's *House of Wisdom*
to the Internet
and *AI*
are wispish constructions
of a Totality
transcending
beginnings and endings

Coiling smoke
evaporating from
the chimneys of the mind
into the nebula
of understanding

Because
splitting the atom
ultimately brings us no closer
to the *Tiamat* of Life and Death
Consciousness
or the meaning of Being
than religion
disco
cubism
boxing
electromagnetism
or any stream
of colorful projections
anxiously washed onto this canvas
of collective dreaming
called *history*

We've created
marvelous things
certainly!

A magnetic *mana*
streams from the minds
of we arrogant apes
flooding this planet

But we've
deluded ourselves
with grandiosity

Our *Icarun* plunge
into an institutionalized
insanity

A naïveté
in trying to capture
the Singularity
behind
the gyration
of Life

Shadow Puppets

Looking back
it all seemed
so *dreamlike*

The ecstatic joys
heart-wrenching betrayals
the large and little moments
shared with all those souls
out to enjoy
the *brief spark*
handed to them
now
only ever felt
like shadow puppets
dreamily prancing behind
the fading curtains
of memory

And the game felt so *real*
until the king
was finally surrounded
surrendering
weak at the knees
as the pieces were gently
redistributed

And all your prayers
were wasted moments
if they didn't teach you

the only prayer
worth answering
was the plea
for patience
strength
integrity
courage
to weather the game
curiously and compassionately
with one foot in the box
knowing all those you encountered
within this *Hydra* of desires
were passing atoms

That each move
was as trivial
as map markings

Because
as all cartographers know
coordinates are only
frames of reference
points on a perceived continuum
absurd without their context

And there was a beauty
and a *saudade*
in realizing
all those hours
were wasted
grieving shadows

Like children
mourning sandcastles
as they return
to find their efforts
reclaimed
by the waves

Agreements

Breathe into uncertainty
Relax into *entropy*

Our truths are *agreements*

And we Exist
in a sea of potentialities
birthed and bound
by thought

Reality is a *perceiving*
and all human understanding
is a reaching toward
that orphic *Shangri-La:*

The path
to unencumbered
authentic Life
emerges through
continuous confrontation
with our reflections
appearing everywhere
we project
attention

Ouroboros

Out of Chaos
find *order*

The strength
to hurl headlong
unguarded
into this
Ouroboric embryo

Serenity
in Creation's Furnace
perpetually spawning
that sacred Trinity:

Knowing
Knower
Known

In peacetime
meditate
on the delights of living
the *Grace* in a smile
healing purity in Animals
and gentle dignity
in authentic Presence

When terror reigns again
draw the sword
with *sabr*

Reflecting
on all the moments
you've wielded it before

Knowing
sometimes
strength must be displayed
courage must be gathered
and difficult periods
must be faced squarely
without hesitation
as it will pull you through
the bleakest nights
and guide others
anxiously wrestling
the dualism
at the essence of *mind*

Through fear
caress humanity
Within desire
observe a neediness
a lack of faith

Let pride and vanity
humble you
exposing the illusions
of your thoughts
your petty cravings
the dichotomy
manifested within everything

meeting your eyes
in this technicolored
reverie

When misery
sends messengers
don't bar the gates
hoping for their
unfulfilled return
to their master

Welcome them
curiously

Allow their songs
to be sung
between your walls
without censor

And at sunrise
send them off
bellies full
always remembering
how it was
to pass the hours
in such *wise* company

The lessons they taught you
The layers behind their stories
as you drank hopelessly
through the night

And remember
how *different* you were
when their horses
were swallowed
by dawn's horizon

How surreal the encounter
How agonizingly beautiful
the gifts
they left by the fire

When Chaos
tears through your Life
see Her rejuvenating power
Her true nature

How all forms
require dissolution
to evolve

Trust
security's
absent in Nature

And anywhere
you're sold
into such a picture

You're alive
but no longer
living

The Scarecrow

Everyday
I see you hobbling
around your tiny balcony
a crutch in one arm
as your other hand
desperately clings
to the rail

Your body
contracting
into a jerky dance
like a scarecrow
lost in the wind

Terrified
that any minute
your arms will relent
and you'll finally understand
you were only ever
a sack of straw
covered with clothes
Existing in a Field
of such *magnificence*
even the birds
gathered at your feet

That this body you've known
since your Mother's Womb
was only a crude casing

around the coil
of eternal Consciousness
that can only be experienced
not explained
by the high priests
of a lost society

I don't know why
Life's broken your body

Why Time
remorselessly takes
what it first gifts
out of pure Love

I can't tell you
why you suffer under the weight
of a heaving maelstrom
of memories
and why your last days
on this mysterious floating sphere
are unrelenting
undignified
contortions

Because
there's a cruelty
to *Māyā*
baffling all who dare
to pry too deeply
into Her shroud

A suffering
that attaches
too well
to the joys of living

A pain
appearing to be
payment for Life
although
we weren't consulted
when the ballots
for the characters
in this spectacle
were drawn
from that
Motherless Hat

And
watching you
I surprisingly feel
the ultimate
justice of Life

I wonder
if you've made Peace with Nature
Peace with the knowledge
that everything you've loved
is being erased
with each hazardous step
as it has for *all*
who've sojourned here

I wonder
if you've managed
to trick the trick of Life
to smile in the face
of this indelible jest
of Creation and Destruction
grinning with graceful cheek
at the marvelous charade
in which you too
have partaken

That painful axiom
oozing
from your lifeless pores
as you carefully
meander that skeleton
around your self-designed
prison

We are guests here
and Life owes us nothing

And it alone
reserves the right
to take what it's given
to punish what it's praised
and to conceal its secret:

Death is Life
in everything
around us

For
regardless
of whether your God
or my God
are on good terms
as they sit playing cards
ceaselessly
in the unmanifested temples
of the mind

I wonder if your suffering
as you've bartered
in this eternal transaction
has taught you
the Magic of living
lies in the transience
of each moment
as it *gallops by*

Experience Itself

We house
both God and Devil
in this dualistic ocean

Ecstasy and bliss
misery and ugliness
the *insanity of war*

Our projections
into this existential spasm
are aspects of Self
a *Lao Tzu* and *Genghis Khan*
dwelling within every human being

Because if Life's purpose
is *experience itself*
then perhaps
its potential meaninglessness
magnifies its magnificence

In the same way
the waves allow the ocean
to experience herself
subjectively
perhaps our lives
are an *adhan*
for the Formless
to comprehend Itself
through form

As I Watched You Bathing

Something
stirred in me
as I watched you bathing
in the *Ganges*

Your young
slender body
relinquishing the *sari*
so naturally
rhythmically
it was as though
you were dancing
out of its clutches

Surrendering your sensuality
to the river
and placing a finger
to the lips
of Time Itself

Forgetting Life
was swirling all around you
A noisy web
of comings and goings
ecstasies and wretchedness

Forgetting
your fragile body
held a power over the world

that's crippled empires
and forged terror
in the hearts of the highest

An alchemic power
that can *create* men
make boys of men
then turn them
into something greater

It was as though
with the release
of each fold of silk
onto those marble steps
delighting
in the momentary kiss of your feet
you were dancing your way
out of the grip
of a stifling society

Returning
to the rhythm
of an archaic drum
beat in these mountains
by your people
long before the great civilizations
were called into the Womb

Before Time and language
When your pristine body
was a phenomenon

of Divinity
worship
curiosity

Not an *object*
to be captured
and exploited
for physical desire
and material profit

And even men like me
who'd roamed freely
under the stars
and among the peoples
of this world
men who'd *fancied*
they'd drunk deeply
of the many sins and desires
of Life's cup
stood embarrassed
shyly peeking through the reeds
in awe and wonder
at the shear natural *power*
of your mysterious Femininity
Your unchartered beauty

Bereft of the thirst
to possess you
own you
but only to worship
at the foot of a *tangible altar*

Marveling red-cheeked
at the beautiful work
of Nature's hand
as it sketched
the curves of your hips
and breathed Grace
into the simple flow
of your movements

As if you
and the water
were one

Childhood friends
embracing
after many years apart

Calling
into question
the linearity
of Time

Something
stirred in me
as I watched you bathing
in the *Ganges*

Mother!

Again
and again
Life after Life
lullabies
sung in ancient tongues
suckling at breasts
the color
of red Earth

Cradled by arms
as dark as charcoal
and loved
nurtured
by a kaleidoscope
of eyes

Mother
Mother!

Where do you go
when the spark of each Life
diminishes?

Where are
your loving glances
your gentle touch
when I breathe my last
in this ferry
of flesh and desires?

And where does your child go
greeting *Charon*
at the shore's edge?

Birth after Birth
I've been soothed
by the songs of our people
only now
reaching the steps
of your *Akashic* temple
yearning
to sit
under your breast
and drink the Truth
flowing through your Love
dream after dream
in every agony
and every bliss

Sing to me
one last time
Mother
and release me
from this
ceaseless
wandering

A Deep Release

Even the most
beautiful face
liveliest smile
harshest tongue
will one-day
be *topsoil*

Life's serious
until it's almost over!

Only then
in that *dreaded dusk*
do we realize
it was never serious
to begin with

That severity
was a specter of thought
and we wasted precious hours
fearing phantoms
that either never materialized
or did
but are now *past*
never as diabolical
as they seemed

For the dying say
living ends *much sooner*
than they'd expected

So
unfurl
into living

When things are good
savor the *trifling moments*
knowing pain
lurks around the corner

And when things are painful
savor them also
for the joyous
will soon be yours
to float in again

Our transitory
joys and sufferings
are not foreign
to all who've come before us

And while sometimes
it appears
you're at the frontier
of uncharted pain
your experiences
are more the norm
than the *exception*

The rule
rather than an anomaly
of this human predicament

Life isn't as serious
as we'd like to imagine

Just realize
where you come from
and let sadness
shape you
into a wellspring
of compassion
for all living things
endlessly swept
into the obscure black
of Eternity

Life's a deep *release*

Create Your Own Culture

Few *live* past twenty-five

Young people
everywhere
throwing their lives
at the feet
of a *maniacal culture*

Consumed
by the ever-spinning
capitalist machine

Selling their souls
for the safety
of supposed security
and a shot at the *cheese*

By thirty
their brains
are marketing mush

Ripe for the picking
by the corporate conglomerates
those guardians of *Gomorrah*
wanting to keep them that way
until their utility's expired

Mushy and malleable
keeps the wheels turning

By seventy
the time some people
begin seeing things
clearly
it's *too late*

Their bodies
are useless
their minds
too narrow
and their lives
too shackled by obligations
to make significant changes

Make your changes *now*
Start *living* now

Burn the boats!

Weave
   your
   personal
      myth

Create your own culture

Raindrops

Hear the drums
Time's *holographic* metronome
vibrating endlessly
through nihility

A Cosmic laughter
echoing
across the vastness
of the Unknown

Use Death to rejuvenate Life

This throat-clearing
of the Creator
arising and vanishing
into Nothingness
in a fractal *lahzeh*

Be content with living
for *we know nothing* of dying

Decay's the nature of materiality
and resistance to its sonorous order
prolongs suffering

Live with morals
not for reward
in suggested realms
but for the pleasure of decency

Enjoy Life
while it lasts
and don't worry
about what comes *next*

We know too little
to waste our days in fear

Confront
that inscrutable
Eleusinian epiphany:

Certainty's
a beguiling
illusion

We are
raindrops rippling
in an incessant
Motherless Torrent

Seek freedom
in the tenuity
of instants

Because the portal
between worlds
opens momentarily

And all of Life
seems a knowing when to *jump!*

Tricks

Careful!

Don't give your coat away
on the first morning
of spring

The winter isn't over
just *hiding*

There's still
more suffering to come
Many joys also

Don't forget:
Sometimes
the Sun
plays tricks
on us

Forgive Her anyway

Keep your coat
and realize
all things
are in the process
of *return*

The Sacred in the Mundane

And what is this circus
of *Being?*

These frayed
phantasmagoric edges
of the living and dying

Can you answer
honestly
when asked
where *you* end
and Life begins?

Does science
your theories clung to
in those desperately certain
hubristic moments
solve the nature of Reality?

Or have you
humbled yourself
to realize certainty's chimerical
culture's the nemesis of Truth
and religion
the hallowed synonym
for politics

Fumbling candles
against the *koan* of Life

This syntactical
Joycean lattice:
Mother Matrix Most Mysterious

An Intelligence so profound
it can only be *felt*
not understood

Embraced by those willing
to hurl their lexicon
into the howling Void
and face the primordial Enigma
naked

If empiricism
folds the answer to Life
in your palm
then tell me why
in our frivolous strivings
have we not edged
a *photon* closer
to grasping the *Ankh*
of Time
Life
Death
dreams
electricity
Love
mathematics
creativity
Consciousness?

Can you quantify
memory
sadness
Awareness
empathy?

And if we could
what would we do
with the knowledge
as one door opens
to an infinite
Shaktic fractal
of unknowing?

The Ineffable
perpetually repelled
by didactics

Sun-soaked camels
attempting to pass
through the eye
of the needle

Because
curiously
like the *Zen* masters
coaxing their students
into Awareness
Life jolts you
in the *minor moments*

Thunderstorms
in the early morning

A shrill scream
in a crowded street

Where
instantly
amid this carnival
of hankerings
and lamentations
you're transported
to a Realm
beyond Time
and language

Pierced
by the sound
of the Interminable
manifesting
and masquerading
as the
mundane

Watch Nature

Spring's proof enough
of resurrection

Three days in a cave
and a unanimous shock:

The grotto's empty of its Messiah!

Beautiful
but unnecessary

Watch Nature
move through the year
Study the lessons
She's yearning to teach

How effortlessly
the flower releases her petals!

Her children
are no longer hers
to cling to

Save your *Hail Mary's*
Drop your *Hare Krishna's*
Consciously observe Nature

Silence cradles more understanding
than countless barren doctrines

Sandcastles

I wanted Life
to pause
in all the *right* places

I wanted
to live
in stories
where I was only
a *minor character*

Until gradually
I began to understand
more experiences awaited
and there were
more lessons
to learn

That
I was only
meant to visit
some rooms
a little while
but the journey
didn't end there

Because
slowly
I recognized that
far from holding me back

Life was carefully
stopping me
from chewing
my mouth

Forcing me
to outgrow
the *comfortable*

Teaching me
some rooms
must be entered
but only *temporarily*

And
in others
we're mysteriously
permitted
to build
sandcastles

Reflections

These words are *reflections*

Scribbling
here and there
in the dead of night
the morning rush
between odd jobs
in tired cafes
on trains
and shaded
park benches

Yet
all these
strange squiggles
dots
and lines
are nothing
but the sounds
of noetics knocking
on the doors
of an inner temple

And the words
are *wajd*
as
aperturally
I remember
where I left my keys!

A Wink

What is this *Thing*
we're engulfed in?

How short
how fragile
are its margins?

How many
hopeful Mothers
proud fathers
desperate disciples
have come
and gone here?

How many
genius's
gurus
messiahs
murderers?

How many tyrants
are *dust*
entwined
with the energy
they vehemently pursued?

How many lovers
united in coital bliss
were certain theirs

was the *love of all loves*
before Time
ravaged their bodies
leaving their story
a susurrus
in the firmament?

Empires
risen and fallen
in the shadows
of mountains
sleeping
since civilization
was a glimmer
in the hungry eyes
of our Ancestors

How many artists
imagined Paradise
before they too
vanished
into the Abyss?

Life's but a wink

The Path Home

Now and then
we need moments of stillness
reflections on Being

Because
even honeymooners
can benefit
from a knock at the door

The room service waiter
unknowingly delivering
a few seconds
to digest Life

And if we look carefully
listen to Intuition's
gentle *zephyr*
we'll notice
that the troughs of our lives
are opportunities
to go *deeper*

That disruptive moments
a traffic jam
a stranger's angry outburst
in a crowded street
a harsh word cast with regret
guide us Home
if we allow it

There
we can soak
in the light
of lost understanding

Will you take
these *chances*
when they arise?

Woman

Woman is the great
Kalic representative
of the Mystery

All balanced cultures
have revered the Feminine
as a manifestation
of the regenerative principle
As guardians of the Unfathomable

Suppression of the Feminine
is an *assault* on Life
an attack on the creative
and an ignorance of Being

The fear of Woman
is a disdain for Existence
A terror of Death

A shivering
neurotic dread
of Nature's stupefying
cyclical power

Because the *Flower of Life*
Aletheia's arcana
lives concealed
in the iridescent *dervish*
of the Feminine

Once More!

So much of Life is *goodbye*

And growing
is learning to part ways
with those whose eyes
we've come to see the world through
with *dignity* and *grace*

For we all part ways
in one way or another
don't we?

That ugly
beautiful
painfully uncomfortable Truth
but *Truth* nonetheless

But connection
shouldn't be avoided
in the face of its temporality

Just as the bee
doesn't fear the flower
whose kiss
seals its demise

But rather
these moments
these *rare windows*

must be embraced
with daring and courage
as we shake
the shackles
of Time
and mortality

And
through
frenzied
painful
grateful defiance
challenge Life:

Once more! Once more!

What Bliss!

What bliss!

Silhouettes
through
the curtains

A dim candle
foreign voices
ancient laughter

Memory so deep
it bites at the heels
of language

The Earth
playfully conceals
Her secrets

But we'll sleep in Her
soon enough

Empty Noise

And when the dust settled
and you reflected
on memory's flux

You realized
how much time was wasted
fighting Life

Because
although you
demanded control
and imagined
you were standing
in the crow's nest
of a vagrant ship
sighting land and smelling sand
on the horizon
you *never knew* what you were doing
who you'd encounter
what yesterday would look like
as it became tomorrow
or who's heart you'd land in

And
as you tried
to beat the Gods
into submission
to the frenetic whims
of your curious mind

you started to see
Life was always moving
along its *own contours*

That you were only ever
the humble plaything
of Cosmic Forces
more ancient
than your Mother's eyes
or the pulsing desire
as the female mind
held a hypnotic charm
over your world
like a dangling rattle

And
wading through
the experiential marshes
you came to comprehend
no one knew too much
either

That music and mathematics
possessed a gravity
A lingering
primeval fragrance
we stumbled across
like teenagers
finding their parent's
photo albums
stuffed behind the cupboard

And that you lost
some of the most
competent navigators
unexpectedly
to the twisting
mysterious reeds
of Life's
lyrical passage

That people
you built a home in
blew it down
with a callousness
that wizened you

And others
who appeared
an unlikely foundation
for longevity
were the first
over the trenches
when the cards toppled
and courage was needed

For
you learned
intelligence and wisdom
rarely dance together
and integrity
isn't as common
as *Aesop* espoused

That Love's
a *seeing*
a reaching toward
the fragility of living

And beauty's a prism
with aesthetics emitting
a dimmer refraction
than you'd once believed

And
in Time
you understood
some things
cannot be replaced
some moments
cannot be recreated
and we can't always
build bridges
between
what once *was*
and what *is*

Because
the more you tasted Life
the greater your appreciation
blossomed into gratitude
for noticing
the *little charms of living*
in the first place

Watching
good people
genuflect
at the feet
of decaying dogmas
you learned that adventure
kept Life *interesting*

And without it
even the brightest souls
slavishly shriveled
like tomatoes
under the Sicilian sun

In Time
you stopped resisting
the deluge
and learned to hurl yourself in
facing whatever was emerging
with appreciation
for the people you'd known
the privileges falling into your lap
like cuttings from *Heka's* paper chain
the experiences
dissolving your assumptions
and curious about
what Life would throw you
at every street corner
where each connection would lead
and in perpetual awe
at the magnificence of the Mystery

the synchronicities of experience
Nature's beauty
and the enduring power
of simple moments
in a world groaning
with *Avidyā*

And even in the darkness
the incandescent glimmers
were so radiant
that you learned
to trust that all of Life's
an undulating succession
of perceptions
causes and effects
yet-to-determine moments
on whose rippled ravines
you lay your thoughts

Surrendering to the same Energy
that gifted sentience
carved the Feminine
and spread the galaxies
like dice
tumbling across the aeons

Knowing sanctity evades us
when sedated
by superficial whims
and nestled gently into the bosom
of an *insane society*

That culture rests
precariously
on hollow ground

The smoke and mirrors
of the venal

That finding harmony
within the Chaos
was the one true
gnosis

And all else
in the face
of our mortal afterthought
was just
empty noise

The Voice in the Void

Don't fear Life

You Are Life
and therefore
you're also Death

As waves
don't fear the ocean
you shouldn't sit in trepidation
of this ineffaceable Flame

One day
you'll merge with it
and realize
there was nothing
to merge into

In the same way
the four winds
only meet in our minds
what you thought was a Death
was just your Mother's voice
calling you
out of a *daydream*

Prison

What is
more important
than tasting Life
with an open heart?

More sacred than *Change?*

We erect the bars
and decorate the prison
yet the door's
wide open

Looking closely
we see:

We're
the jailed
jailing
the jailer

And
our problems
tremble
at
the
feet
of
Death

Living is Relationship

This living
is a *relationship*

We Exist relative
to other nexus points

An infinity
of perspectives
radiating through a medium
of pure potentiality

Each point
depending
on its *context*

So
why's my perspective
so important?

How can my God
my happiness
my *truth*
reign above
all other points?

How accurate
a reflection of Reality
is my node
in this *Ensō?*

And how could my lens
ever reflect
the Totality
of experience?

When was the last time
you connected
with the moment?

With the *Absurd*
that pulsing
vibrating chasm
between past and future?

Connected such
that you were certain
you'd gathered
enough pure input
to discern locality
causality
ethics?

Such that you'd dissolved
ideas and linguistics
boundaries between forms?

Where the futilities
of our collective ambitions
kneel at the steps of a *Quintessence*
so incomprehensible
your thought agreements evaporate

We are projections
floating through
a soup of *Sapna*

Sleepwalkers
from the *Non-Euclidean*
driven by our thoughts
and *imprisoned*
by our choices

An ocean of faces
bookended
between the vacuum

We could Be
so much more
do so much more!

Capable of birthing
democracy
da Vinci's
calculus
quantum mechanics
Omar Khayyam's
Maya Angelou's
Plato's
Tesla's
yet we settle
for the debased
manipulative concoctions
of the insipid!

What's the noblest principle
worth striving for?

Could you pursue it
at the cost
of security and respect?

Can you see
perfection's an *ideal*
yet in striving
reaching for the Impervious
we meet with the Gods?

Can you taste true Presence
Be without *becoming?*

Discern Godliness
manifesting
in these prostituted streets
intoxicating in its breath
when it draws near?

Or have you been too long
without sustenance
that you're satiated
by *crumbs?*

In its absence
can you cherish
the memory
of the Sublime?

Devote your Life force
to respecting the Numinous?

Or are you content to hide
in the pettiness
of our cultural charade?

The blank spaces
carved out for you
by the vacuously vacant

Buried under
the syntactical weight
of a *terrified species*

Do we see Life
as it *Is*
or as we *are?*

And if we cannot know
what we *are*
how can we *dare*
to declare Truth?

Do you see this flutter?

The shouts of the ignorant
from the rooftops
as the wise
watch this *khayal*
pass away

Kings and the destitute
sinners and saints
trembling
before the magnitude
of this Thing!

All eventually enveloped
by the Cosmic whitewash

The light and darkness
of civilization
but the birdsong
in a universal dawn

How deep
need we go
before knowing
needs from wants
fears from choices?

How do past and future
influence our present?

And where
do you define
the individual
and the collective?

Do we create Reality
or are fate and free will
roommates?

This living is a duality
a juggling act

Experience
a *feedback*

A tremor
reverberating
through the fabric
of Time-space

And
we Exist
only
in relationship

Mirrors

Stillness coaxes
Intuition's
subtle Truth

Divinity
cannot be
imprisoned
in rite or ritual

Have the courage
to seek *Ayn al-Qalb*
alone

Inspiration befriends
the seraphic
as the *Grail* unveiled
for *Galahad*
and *Excalibur*
spurned sheep

Remember those words
carved over the doorway
in *Delphic* stone:

Know Thyself

The temple walls
are filled
with mirrors

And Life's
a curious flux
between
timing
and
patience

Dualities

Until you can accept
that you *too*
are capable
of insidious evil

That a Hitler
and a Christ
live in each of us

That history's stained
with an aggregate of
unfathomable violence

And that beauty
can be found
in the church
and the brothel

Your piety's worthless
goodness hollow
and morality
a delusion

A hypocritical sophistry
cloaking cowardice

Courage

Courage is learned
by plunging into the fire
and emerging from the ashes
burnt
but
braver

Only Life teaches courage
You won't learn it
in school
church
or by emulating heroes

Courage is a *solitary* pursuit
A *Hajj* of harrowed edges
and uncertainty

But knowing
you can face Life unblinking
trembling
as the Unknowable
engulfs you

Knowing sleeping's easier
but choosing to wake
to another day in *Hell*
because you trust in your strength
is the ultimate gift
of the *Empyrean*

All We Had Was Time

And your words tasted
like they were
chiseled
in *Gizan* lime

As you drifted
to a Sunday
in the hills together

The first time
he conceded
among the crickets
and eucalyptus
marinating the bitumen
that the beautiful moments
would be *numbered*

That first day
you grasped
a Life
forever altered

That this
man and mind
would be mote again
in a matter of months

Whatever that meant

Despite
the *Christian Science* magazines
strewn desperately
around your bedroom floor
near the bloody tissues
stuffed in hidden corners
that you'd silently collect

A secret transaction
neither of you'd verbalize

Because
nothing could have
prepared you
for that Truth

And all the religions
on this conflicted planet
all the well-intended advice
about *just-getting-on-with-it*
from those stoic
war-hardened elders

All the optimistic
boyish certainty of youth
the artistic movements
the heavy
candid philosophical talks
of Life and Death
drenched in smoke
and the fondue

gently hardening in the morning light
the cards and backgammon
as one decade
merged into another
girlfriend became wife
wife became Mother
revolutions were won and lost
in foreign lands
women traded miniskirts for *burqas*
Nixon warred on drugs
and geniuses overdosed
in Greenwich studios

All the king's horses
and all the king's men
couldn't prepare you
for the coldness of his skin
and the stiffness of his hands
as *true to his word*
he became memory

A lingering
ghostly signature
on the mortgage

And your mind
clung to words and phrases
he'd said

Gently filtering reality
from dreams

The person he *was*
from the person
he was *becoming*

As his watch
ticked away
on your son's wrist
who'd apparently
become a man
in the years
since the diagnosis

An awful
agonizing reminder
that this world
stops for no one

And I asked
if the years
had changed your perspective
of the man you knew

If Time
had colored
youth's stills
with a different hue

It's clearer
you replied

Clearer!

As you were now
thrice the age you were
on that beautiful Sunday

As you'd seen
grandchildren
and marriages dissolve

Found Love
and widowhood *again*

Watched wars ignite and smolder
the world swivel anxiously
on fingertips in a Soviet bunker
regimes and maps shuffle
the rise of the Internet and the Islamic State
and the year 2000 arrive
as unceremoniously as any other
while the doomsday fanatics
folded their *Mayan Calendars*
returning resentfully
to their desks
in the new millennium
with a little more work
and a little less Life

It's clearer

Those words
the only evidence I'll need
to discard with Time's vector

To digest
the kinesis
of Life

The mystic *Merkaba*
at the skirt
of sense and intuition
endlessly en route
to becoming memory

Another Universe
rustled and awoken
in some unknown future when
wandering through
the vaporous *brane* of possibilities
we gaze across
the chiaroscuro of our lives
realizing
that against
the throbbing throng
of trivialities
all we ever had
was Time

Hostages

I dream of how it was
before advertising
stole our gratitude
and sold us
perfection

Before social media
convinced us
masks guaranteed love
and Hollywood brainwashed us
into exposing
every part of ourselves

Celebrating
our imperfections

Distinguishing between
needs and *wants*

Knowing true beauty's
vulnerability

Is thrusting the lance
into the Dragon
imprisoning Truth
in the highest tower
of this mysterious
dreamscape

Beauty Isn't Everything

You're beautiful
and your face turns heads
in every street
but is your mind as seductive
as your smile?

People melt at your glance
yet does your soul *burn*
with a yearning
for Truth?

The way you move's a dance
a floating
on the crest of Life

Yet who *are* You
waking at night
staring into darkness?

Who *are* You
in the Emptiness
between moments?

Have you ventured
to comfort's edge?

Had the courage
to leap into the chasm
of your inadequacies?

Stared into fear
quivering
and chosen Love?

Your beauty opens doors
in every city

But I wonder
if you've dared to knock
on the doors
of your subconscious

To feel
who You *are*
behind *names* and *forms?*

There's a power
in the way you move your lips
and you know it

But how often
do you use those lips
to pull others out of pain?

To walk beside them
in their *dukkha?*

To talk only
of Peace and Love
as if they were
old school friends?

Have you been crushed
by Life's injustices
yet climbed out of misery
unguarded?

Your naked body
breaks the most powerful people
but I want to witness
your integrity
when compromised

How are
your foundations
when shaken
by the allure and promises
of the world?

Your beauty's
undeniable
sirenic
mysterious

But
your beauty
without character
is the
ugliest thing
in the world

We've Lost Ourselves in Names

We've lost ourselves in names

Created barriers
between our Awareness
and the humming
terrifying *Aliveness*
around us

Allah
  God
    Brahman
     Yahweh
      Source
     Energy
  Universe
Tao

We've forgotten
these are
interchangeable
symbols

Fingers
pointing toward
the Ungraspable

Names
have divided us
semantics *corrupts*

Our *beliefs*
put the certainty
on our lips
and the hatred
in our hearts

Yet the *Essence remains*

Each name's
a door
to the same House

We've heard
science without spirituality
is a deadened road
and spirituality without science
detaches us from Life

Yet perhaps
science and spirituality
are *ancient lovers*
desperately reaching
for each other

And we
foolishly strive
like fearful parents
to keep them
apart

Breathe

When you doubt yourself
breathe
Feel your heartbeat
Release your bare feet into Nature
and listen to the primordial whir
of Her aeonic resonance

It will reconnect you
to the *Mandala* of Life
the *ghumūḍ al-ḥayāh*
you're inseparable from

A permeating
Intelligence
beyond
comprehension

That wisdom
disguised
in endless tongues
and endowed to the *Pharisees:*

*The Kingdom of Heaven
is within*

And perhaps
you'll finally
trust it

Ephemeral Creatures

And then there are the days
where the sky
coaxes you into a smile
like the memory
of an old lover

And those boats
glide through the canals
carrying the hopes
of all of us ephemeral creatures
passing shortly under this ray of forms
Drinking and singing
in irreverent honesty
A true sexuality
like those early Elvis records
before the world cashed in
on their golden goose
proving
sometimes
beauty's safe
only in obscurity

That we cheapen Life by defining it

And that
true joy's granted
only in those rare windows
intangibly falling between
past and *future*

Something Deeper

Tell me about *You*
not your situation
job
friends

Tell me about
your hopes
fears
dreams

Those moments
you can't bear your reflection

The mornings you arise
feeling you're
going through the motions
because you've more to offer this world
of heaving ideologies
and awkward hypocrisies

That there's something more
something deeper

An intangible dimension
behind the prosaic
you swear lurks
beneath every thought
arriving in your palm
at the edge of the *Abyss*

Tell me about
your most ecstatic sexual experience
deepest love
greatest betrayal
the one thing you'd change
if you could

Divulge the visions
that snuck away

Show me
your naked Self
the *You behind the you*
the child
longing for Love
from this fragile world

How far can you go
before you start
to *shiver*
to doubt your center?

How long
can you marinate in insecurity
before surrendering into a sea
of *cymatics?*

Before you realize
control's illusory
experience unending
desire *ephemeral*

The *trust*
that whatever Life *Is*
it's carried you
since you left the Womb
and perhaps
it will carry you
further still

How far
can you fall
before you *beg*
for salvation?

Before doubt
creeps into your mind
like an unwanted vine?

What gnaws at the brink
of your Awareness?

What keeps you up
listening to music all night?

What *Dionysian* urge
sees you reach
for the next glass
bed the next body?

How many experiences
have you tasted
seeking the root of Being?

How many times
have you loved
without climax
and how many
sexual partners?

Because every experience
every momentary lover
has only pushed me
further
into the inscrutability
of living

Posed more *questions*
than answers

And
how would you
change society
if you could
for one day?

Do you think
Herculean souls
are born or made?

What do you think
of Love
Life
Death
God?

Is sound
the cause or effect
of Creation?
Or *both*?

Are we victims
or victors
here?

What do you ache for?

And what
are you willing to do
to get it?

Now tell me:

Against infinity's
monstrous echo
have you realized
certitude's
a beautiful
temptress

But
  she
    can't
  be
    found
   in
    Nature

Under the Moonlight

Not quite Gods
not quite animals

We're
cognizant of Death
yet powerless
to change it

We reach
for the Unreachable
while murdering
in the name
of *Truth*

The awkwardness
of our human dilemma
should bond us
in compassion

The shocking
brevity
of our experience
should unite us
like prisoners
scheming escape
under the moonlight

But it doesn't

We slaughter each other
over *objects*
condemning Peace
over *Barabbas*

And
when morning comes
the door opens
and our toys
are *returned*
we realize
the world wasn't
a *mercenary*
sent to harm us

Rather
a blissfully indifferent host
who invited us
to a mesmeric gala
and wasn't bothered
if we slipped out
before midnight

As memory
and *monad* merge
we see the pain we inflicted
was the *hemlock*
dripping
down
our
throats

Lessons

Life *appears* to be
a series of lessons
cloaked as suffering
forcing you
to drop your walls
and open your heart

Fear
followed *Faust*
until he faced her
fluid forms

She cannot be avoided *forever*

The seeker accepts
there's a lesson
in every moment
even if its meaning
hides within
the web of Life

Confront your darkness
and you may find
an apparition

A *banshee*
beneath the bed
waiting to be dissolved
by the light

For Truth

Words are shadows of stillness

Semantic signposts
on the road
to *Shambhala*

Totems draped
over the perplexity of Truth

Yet for Truth
I'd *unlearn language*
abandoning syntax
to remember how it was
loving the world
without conditions

Before the sky
was a *three-letter word*
and words
were a clumsy attempt
at *knowing*

So
take these shadows
and feel joined to *living*
like a Mother
placing her hand
        on the *kick*
of her unborn child

Scarred

You aren't crazy
just scarred

And we're all a little scarred
in a world seduced
by separation

But you shouldn't run
from your scars

Run towards them
into them
beyond them

Until you realize
Life scars all
who open their hearts
enough

Not all baggage
is a burden

And scarred
doesn't mean
useless

That damage
creates character
Charm

And although
it's a nice daydream
we wouldn't want
to pass through Life
untouched

It would be
spitting
on the doors
of *Olympus*

Love yourself
and love your cracks

They're proof
of your courage
to live *unguarded*

A sign
Life's opened you
like a lotus
and
disguising Itself
as a beggar
pleaded with you
not to close over

This Culture is Not Your Friend

This culture
is not your friend

It is designed
by clever people
egoic cowards
to make you feel *inferior*

Whole people
don't consume trash
incomplete people
can't stop buying

See past
the bread and circuses

Understand the psychology
behind this consumerist
merry-go-round

This ugly market
seeking to *set your value*

We are *Magick* manifested!

A synchronicity
surpassing mind and matter
that cannot be diluted
by draconian opiates

Reclaim your dignity
your beauty
your infinite luminescence
as a *Ruh*
traversing
this sacred planet

Just Possibilities

All religions
corrupted
when their possibilities
became *Truths*

And I distrust anyone
monopolizing Truth
over possibility

No one guards Truth
simply potential roads
to the *Etz Chaim*

And we know too little
to reject or defend
roads attempting
to deliver us there

Keep each teaching
as a *possibility*
and you'll saunter through Life
seeing divinity diffused
in every atom

Truth exists somewhere
but as long as you're
submersed in this *Dunya*
you'll create violence
declaring you've found it!

True Masculinity

We've *betrayed* our sons

Sold them
a distorted
manhood

True masculinity's
a gentle respect for Life
strength facing fear
and courage to speak Truth
in a world paying handsomely
for lies

Masculinity
is knowing
strength's an obligation
to care for *all creatures*
not an opportunity
to control them

Despite what we've told our sons
masculinity isn't dominion

Money doesn't maketh the man
power doesn't maketh the man
nor do sexual conquests
or an aloof indifference
our idols
endearingly exude

True manhood
is confronting Life's sufferings
with integrity

Respecting
the sacredness
of the *Feminine principle*
in ourselves
in women
and in Nature

It's seeing beauty
in every person
and striving
through words and deeds
to leave this planet
a better place

We've *failed* our sons
where we should've guided them
into the landscape
of authentic masculinity

We've abandoned our boys
and ceded power
to a culture
unconcerned with producing
decent men
and hellbent
on turning people
into *commodities*

This Strange Dream

Jumping quickly
into bed
I think of all of you
sleeping in shop alcoves
and freezing concrete pavements

Stuffed away fetally
in busy city side streets
like used toys in the attic

Stoned to sleep
and soaked
in spirits and sadness

Imagining
somewhere
you know you're adored
and your suffering
isn't *unnoticed*

I try to meet your eyes
and when I don't
I meet them in my thoughts

Because
I hear your loneliness
your despair
at the inequity
of this depraved hoax

And after
I lie there grateful
realizing
a warm bed
and a good book
are *privileges*
denied to many

That safety's
underappreciated

And that
at a mere toss
of the astral dice
we could've
traded places

So
tonight
as the trams
rattle
through winter

I send you
Love
light
and the strength
to wake
to another day
in this
strange dream

The Keys to Canaan

It's human
to seek Providence
when fortune wanes
isn't it?

We've all felt it

Nothing's crazy
when you're
prostrating
begging
hoping
something's *listening*

But when
Life's working out
and we're on
the winning ticket
we relinquish our talismans

We forget
our Divinity
and the Forces
guiding us

For it's only
falling into the well
that we pray for someone
to throw down a rope

Only within the whale
that *Jonah*
found humility

Perhaps
the desperate moments
are signals

Encounters with Spirit

Without them
we'd be transfixed
by trivialities
neglecting the wonder
surrounding us
That is us

Paradoxically
the hardest moments
mask beautiful gifts

Invitations
to relinquish conditionality
and recognize and return *Home*

More precious
than worldly pleasures
and an unblemished Life

Because pain
creates *depth*

And depth
invokes an openness
to beauty's infinite forms

And once beauty
surrounds you
even pain
transfigures

And Life
finally confers
the keys
to *Canaan*

Alive

Eventually
you'll wake to a morning
where you realize
you feel *good*

That you've been
feeling good
for a while now

That the places which *seared*
now house a dull aching

Traces of stories
unfolding
somewhere out there

And the painful memories
feel more like dreams
like *past lives*
than Reality

And curiously
one of Life's
hardest observations
is finding that
impermanence means
our suffering too
fades into the misty *Yantra*
of memory

Because we become so familiar
with our pain
we identify with it

And like a bad hangover
we forget how it felt
to be free of agony

We forget
even suffering's
a transitory guest

And when we emerge
from the solitary path
pain creeps out the back door
if we leave it unlocked
and Life lights
the road forward
if we trust it

And one day
you'll be liberated
by the realization
that you finally traversed *Hell*
and arrived on the other shore
knowing that
even if you *wanted*
to retrace your steps
and follow the breadcrumbs back
to who you once were
you couldn't find your way

Because you aren't
the same person
who stepped
terrified
into the fire
all those years ago

You're
scarred
burnt
different

But Alive
very much Alive

This Sludgy Maze of Perspectives

In the end
what *truly matters*
considering how quickly
we're ripped from this world?

How soon
this flash of Consciousness
is extinguished
and the echoes of the masses
evaporate into etheric memory

Because we digest Life
through reductive valves

And perhaps
like *Arjuna* beholding *Krishna's* true form
Moses quivering by the *Burning Bush*
Buddha under the *Bodhi* tree
the narrowness of our daily awareness
is a necessary insulator
against the *Sublime*

And while our perceptive filters
navigate the sociocultural landscape
they blur
the most *arcane* truths

These profound realizations
such as the *brevity* of our mortality

are naturally undesirable meditations
amid a whirlwind of supermarket trips
sexual encounters
and family milestones

But isn't it *curious*
that the central tenet
of all spiritual practices
is the ego's disintegration
and surrender to a Higher Power
than our intellect?

A death of waking Consciousness
and a reconnection
to the *Spout of Life*

Because
when gifted a moment
to digest our eventual dissolution
we recognize that
contrary to the delusional
subtextual narratives
espoused by modern society
we're all steadily marching
towards the grave

Against this
what is Change
judgment
ostracization
vanity?

Faced with
the *startling shortness* of Life
the fact that
every beating heart
will cease
in little over a century
what's a single
compelling
endurable reason
not to pursue
our deepest desires?

To discard society's whims
and submit to the silent magnetism
of Intuition?

We've conditioned ourselves to stay small

We bathe in the fears of others
carrying the products
and putrefying beliefs
of people and institutions
we couldn't care less about

We permit people's
self-protecting masks
to lord their power over us
forgetting
those we feel judged and diminished by
are carried relentlessly and helplessly
by the same Current

That *no one's got a clue*
what's going on here
despite the protean
masquerades and accolades
we drape over each other

Therefore
the purest self-love
is reflecting on the magnitude
of Existence

That we arrive from
and return to
an Unknown
that cannot be
dismissed and sedated
by a panacea of *Flavian* Super Bowls
and Golden Globes

If pursued with courageous
reckless abandon
we realize Life's a *daring jump*
and we're enslaved and freed
by our beliefs

Everything and *nothing* matters
simultaneously!

And we navigate our experience
through the sludgy maze of perspectives
not *Truth*

Far Too Late

When Life gifts glimpses
we shouldn't fear
the terrifying shadow it casts
but surrender to the obscure
trusting that
whatever path our story takes
it can lead to serenity
if we allow it

Because so much of Life
is a *letting go*
something we each confront
greeting this *Janus* like an old friend
or dragged kicking and screaming
from the things
we once knew and loved

Yet Life grants us moments
windows to act with grace
and these windows
don't stay open
forever

But
   the wind
          carries
     Simorgh
       to our door
far too late

Embrace Silence

Embrace silence
Don't run from it
like our culture
encourages you to
at every corner

Be prepared to enter
the *Kalic* Mystery of Life
through the threshold
of direct experience
not as a curious onlooker
in the various
didactic charades
you've been taught to master
since *Knossos's* fall

Don't outsource Truth!

Society wants you
incoherent and docile
adrift in an airy maze
of *Thou Shalts*
yet the emperor's *naked*

Silence refines perception
Find your center
and let it guide you
to effortless action

Nature pursues the path
of least resistance

A *wu wei*
longing to reunite
with Intuition

And thought's
a shadow
lost within the Sun

From the Inside

All necessary revolutions
must be preceded
by *inner* transformation

A transfiguration
in individual cognizance
will inevitably alter our species'
perception of Life

No one
who's plumed the depths
of their *biophilic* Being
can harm the Earth
or any creature
birthed from Her
for it would be
self-harm

All systems evolve
from within

Hades' boon
to *Persephone*
and that *Hermetic* law
resounding through Nature's
entangled symphony:

As above
so below

Play

We've been duped
by the fallacy
that living must be *serious*

That play's
for children
artists
the elderly

The otherworldly
and anti-utilitarian
useless in a society
drowning
in economic
and military might

By school
our perceptions
are carefully curated
by teachers
parents
peers
priests

A succession
of *regurgitated*
Life-fearing agendas
moralities
and judgments

Guilt creeps in
play becomes a *reward*
not a state
and we begin to feel
the retreat of childhood's
whimsical *multiverse*

A perturbed
unworthy
anamnesis

We're indoctrinated
into a paradigm
of play as a
consolation prize
for hard work

By adolescence
we're instructed
into complete subordination
to a system worshipping
competitiveness
and conformity
where
the non-adulating
the non-adhering
are outcasts

By twenty
childhood's
pointlessly imaginative play

141

has been channeled
into a vertigo of distractions
and sedations

Play's relegated
to the underdeveloped
and the *feminine*
both undesirable
in a society exalting
aggression
and cohesive submission

We're increasingly
handed demeaning
dehumanizing value structures
serving as *control icons*

Trampling each other
to garner respect
from the apathetic
neurotic
cultural masthead

By adulthood
play's foreign
archaic
clumsy

An *Edenic* memory
morphed into culturally certified
apparitions

We glimpse children
exploring the world
and feel a rousing itch
that perhaps
we lost something

Perhaps we've
blindly swallowed
a reductionism
desperate
to conquer and claim

To do rather than *Be*
To know rather than *wonder*

Because
the industrial model thrives
on Time's *perceived linearity*

It's conveniently dispelled
the cyclical model
of preexisting cultures
to exert a monopoly
on Reality

Linearity
drives productivity
economies and excess
and Life's defamed
and defined
by measurable periods

that can be monitored
and extracted
for profit

Anything but Time
as *progressive action*
is lazy and wasteful

Being without doing
is a childish indulgence
a selfish departure
from the responsibilities
of citizenship

We're ensured
play's for the drifters
the *Peter Pans*
Pariahs awash
in aimless appreciation
of the petty and puerile

Degenerates
refusing to salute
society's flag
and digest its
lethic nectar

Yet
it's obvious
Indigenous cultures
revered play

Work
was Life-sustaining
but play
was *Life-affirming*

A union
with the cyclicality of Creation
the fugacity of *Chitta*
and the fertility
of their deities

Play was tantamount
to touching the
meaningless fecundity
of Life

Childhood's *ambrosia*
was revealed to
and revered in
the *Shamans* and Elders
the cultural gatekeepers
of reverence

Venerated
leaders who'd traversed
the Life cycle
touched the *Dreamtime*
and redeemed the childlike
boon of *Being*

We've been told we're periphery!

Alienated from our roots

Convinced
our passions and talents
are only worthy
when monetizing
social standing

Yet
in slaughtering play
we've denied rapture
at the complexities
of a *chrysanthemum*
the brilliance of an iris

We've slayed
the *djinn* of novelty
the potency of the Other

Life's heady
healing tonic

We've
    buried
  the
    sunflowers
       at
         the
     end
        of
         Time

The Unseen Reaches for Us All

All forms
fall prey to Nature
eventually

But some
are reclaimed
far sooner
than we'd hoped

No matter
how desperately
we cling to the window frames
and rattle our bells in the hallway
flashing photographs
of moments
and sliding memories
under the door
to *Shades*

But perhaps
that's *not a bad thing*

Perhaps
we need the anguish of loss
to touch the quiddity
of being a living
breathing
sentient creature
on this painfully beautiful planet

Because
nothing is immovable
under Time's beating wings

And Change
is the imperishable constant

That Truth
the greatest minds
to witness this sunrise
have eventually
conceded to

The realization
that perhaps Life
isn't meant to be clung to
or understood
simply lived

That *Amba*
of all religion
art
science

Concoctions peppering history
Our collective abstraction

Because
we're not here
to predict futures
and perfect the past

Life's lived
forwards

And all forms
should be savored
but gracefully relinquished
when the tide returns
to reclaim her blessing

Because people
lose precious Time
at the feet of ghosts
who've left the building
long before they finally
board up the doors

And even
a joyous moment
on this fleeting *Odyssey*
is defiant proof
that you lived and loved and lost
and lived and loved and lost *again*

No small thing
in a world teeming with
inexplicable despair

So
feel your pain
and watch it eventually
pass through you

Because we all hand
the things we love
back to Life
sooner or later

But don't allow
the *toska* of living
the transitory agonies of this riddle
to harden your heart
and invite cynics
to dine at your table

Because shedding naïveté
isn't cynicism

And losing faith
is only ever meant to be
the leaving of your shoes
at *Sinai's* steps

The genesis
of the *Fool's Journey*
not the end

Be thankful for your memories
grateful for the lessons
marveling at the privilege
of sharing but a moment
in this infinite play
of Cosmic novelty
with another *chayah*

Behold
the horizon
with the excitement
and trepidation
of all daring travelers
bound for dissolution

Beautiful or ugly
as moment
morphs into memory
the Unseen
  reaches
for us all

Ripples

Amid pain
find beauty

At the center of *Hell*
find God

At the crossroads
of your Life
sit a moment
observe your mind
feel the confusion
in your footsteps
and listen
to that Eternal Compass
dormant in your navel

There's an Intelligence
within us
confounding
the *Cartesian*

A *Vesica Piscis*
of spirit and substance

A wisdom laughing at words

And like all natural phenomena
it strengthens if we feed it
and withers if we don't

For we're all faced
with choices

Moments
creating *ripples*

Grooves
in the fabric
of destiny

And integrity
isn't always
a gentle path

Its stones aren't as worn
trees aren't as manicured
and the horizon
looks dark and lonely

Yet
honoring Intuition
acting instinctively
and perceiving with equanimity
are insurrections
in an acutely
sick society

Ebbs and Flows

The political
economic
and sociocultural structures
of the West
are *crumbling*

We've allowed
the human experience
to be cheapened
defamed
by disingenuous puppets
of shadowy power structures
in these *last days of history*

Life's been robbed
of its Mystery

Nature's been robbed
of its sacredness

Pain's been robbed
of its transformative quality

We've been sold the lie
of Life as a perpetual progress

Yet where does the tide surge infinitely?
Where does the wind howl
or the Sun shine without end?

Nature reminds us
Life ebbs and flows
cyclically
something our culture's
fixated on disguising
while withering
under the same *law*

We can't look twenty-five at sixty
simply because
all forms dissolve
and we too are forms
ensnared
in this labyrinth

Yet
we continue
to beg the Gods
to grant us a second youth
a smile that never fades
and a Life without suffering

We seek permanence
in a traveling circus

And refusing
the ebbs in Life
is the dangerous side-effect
of a culture
obsessed
with progress

Our search for novelty
has led us to a familiar scene:

That primeval search
for the *Fountain of Youth*
sold endlessly
in ever-evolving packaging

For our society
denigrates momentary stasis

We deny ourselves *Ma*
temporary confusion
or existential lulls

Look closely!
We're addicted
to our projections

Bathing in an anxious malaise
of indeterminable futures
we find anything
to avoid Life's natural *troughs*

But Nature
watching our pitiful
Tower of Babel
patiently teaches us
no organism
thrives permanently
She doesn't allow it

Every form
requires recalibration

Action and non-action

And it's this
dualistic cadence
between sempiternal forces
effortlessly
sustaining Life
ex nihilo

An Echo into the Abyss

And when it's all said and done
and the pawns and kings
return to the same box
what will we lament?

Where will our minds wander
waking
from this fog
of form and shadow?

Will we finally see
the majesty of Life
of Breath
of Being?

Relinquishing our body to *Gaia*
will we see the Magic
forever present
in the simple moments?

The immortal reverberation
in the silence
between thoughts

Sighing in curious humility
at the realization
that the sacred
was always
in the quotidian

A smile
laughter
the warmth of a lover's body
tender moments
between old friends
generosity between strangers

Will we finally see
Life was never meant to be
a *striving*
a pursuing
a desperate clutching
for security and power
but a surrender?

That all anyone
ever wanted
was *Love*
the freedom to Birth
a unique expression of Reality

As thought disperses
will we see the foolishness
of our obsession with control?

That something Ineffable animates
A *Rosa Mystica*
foolishly resigned
to pomp and politics
denigrated by dogma
and Leviathan whimsicality

And what of
Agape
charity
friendship
as the frontiers
of this *Prajapatic* plane
begin to undulate?

Will we
cling to resentment
or shed our attachments
to particle and wave?

As our story ends
and we begin to peer
through *Māyā's* looking glass
will we face the elliptic
gracefully succumbing
to annihilation?

And when
the static of Awareness
transmutes
and you feel the timeless pull
ending empires and galaxies
will you go willingly?

Or will you yearn for the old days
nostalgic moments long past
people and places you adored
stories you once inhabited?

We are fractals
of the Divine

Frequencies
in a toroidal field

And Life's
an echo
into *the Abyss*

A Tender, Nirvanic Moment

The *Upanishads*
name the Supreme
creative principle
the Ultimate Reality
Brahman

The indestructible Bliss
permeating Existence
beyond conception

The Changeless Changer of Change

And I've often thought of *Love*
as much the same

It's always struck me
as uncomfortably curious
how often Love's been used
as a synonym for God
across the pages
of all religions
philosophies
mythologies
and works of art

Perhaps
it's because
both Love and God
remain Mysteries

in a world deluded
by arrogance and ignorance

A society *certain*
it can uncover
the root
of every phenomenon

Yet these two
elusive *Titans*
evade us perpetually

Perhaps it's because
both Love and God
require a leap of faith

A plunge into the abstract

The ultimate contact
with ourselves and another

The bliss and ugliness
of the human experience

The majesty
of the Mystery

For I'm not too sure
about a Heaven and *Hell*
Milk and honey
and all that

Infinite incarnations
of avatars
in otherworldly realms

To me
it doesn't much matter

We live through
so many versions of each
find so many lives
within this existential blink
know *too many faces*
that I've come to suspect
we carry both
within us

And I'm certain
many eyes
have witnessed
the unspeakable

Yet in some
there's a rare spark
birthed at the confluence
of suffering and sensitivity
gifted only to those
incapable of feeling the world
as anything
but an extension
of *Self*

This I believe to be
the peculiar gift
granted
to the explorers
of all that is True and beautiful
in the creative landscape
of our collective psyche

All that is graceful
and authentic
in Life

For the meek
shall supposedly
inherit the Earth

But my guess
is the word *meek*
was lost somewhere
in the two thousand years
between the lips
of those barefoot prophets
and the towering
perverted monopolies
of Europe

Perhaps *meek*
was intended to mean
the gentle
the perceptive
the pure of intent

Those who can discover
that ray of beauty
that crack
between two unfathomable doors
Existing within each moment

The subtle gems
of living in a world
riddled with unimaginable
and *unavoidable* suffering

The jewel in the lotus
Oṃ maṇi padme hūṁ
as the Buddhists
so beautifully put it

Because
this sensitivity
bequeaths entry
into both doors

The agony and the ecstasy
cloaked as blessing and burden

And this edge of darkness
feels *insurmountable* at times
but what is Life without Death?

What is Life
if not a daily dying
to the person we once were?

To the shackles
of insincere ideologies
vapid opinions
and outdated modes of being

Trivializing
all we deemed important
as we polish the mirror
watching the superficialities melt away
uncovering our purest manifestation

So
confronted by Death
don't dim your incredible *nūr*
your curiosity
your Essence

Let it burn
free from memory and mind
illuminating all it contacts

Above all
have *faith*

Faith in yourself
faith in Life
and faith
that *light* can be found
in the darkest places
should we pursue it
with dignity and courage

Seek to be
a tender
nirvanic moment
in a kaleidoscope
of color and Chaos

Because
even a moment
between curious
and sensitive minds

A moment in awe
of Life's majesty
in a circus ending
just as we learn
how to juggle

Is enough
of a treasure
to account for *Existence*

Be Your Own Oasis

Be your own oasis!

Create your own Reality
rather than have it filtered
by a culture
disinterested in enlightening you

Christ Consciousness
cannot be commanded
by Papal pageantry

No-thing
will make you happy
until you allow happiness
that *mysterious rogue jester*
a room in your castle

Happiness
a deadened word
is a *forgoing* of form
and a surrender
to Life unfolding

Everything you've wanted
will bring misery
until happiness is a *shedding*
not a gaining

Revealing a *childish* spontaneity

Don't Try to Control the Wind

We seek
memory's refuge
when confusion
stalks our shadow
like a hungry street dog

We cling
to archaic beliefs
stale emotions
and borrowed arbitrations
because it's more comforting
than torching
the boats of memory
and watching all that *was*
evaporate
into a marmoris
of causation

An inextricable web
of experiences

But we want control
power over
the Omnipotent

A Force
only understood
through metaphors
and pointed fingers

My lips
are moving
but my
words
   bring
      us
         no
            closer
               to *knowing*

For
I've no proof
simply an openness
to the *Ungraspable*
living in each breath
behind each blink
and the roaring Emptiness
between moments

Because
banishing Chaos
from our experience
is a *fantasy*
reducing our lives
to a series
of contrived encounters
and projections

Life softens
when we allow
this Phenomenon

to experience Itself
through us

Welcoming Providence
and embracing Change
as it shakes the roots
of our most vehement convictions
molding us
into beautifully
fallible creatures

Don't try
to control the wind

Let it rattle
sense out of Self
laughing
at our fruitless grasping
for control

Our perennial
reaching for the reins
of this fugitive horse
furiously galloping
into *Abraxas*
to meet
its Master

This Aeonic River

Everlasting Peace
is a noble *drishti*
as we cycle through
these contortions of craving
but not entirely possible
in these streets
where we lovers meet
part
and roll on
through the oscillations of living

Perhaps
Peace isn't cultivated
but *reunited* with
as wading through
the restless moments
we yield to the impalpability
of Existing between
two infinitely confounding certainties:

Birth and *Death*

Amid these megalithic portals
what is pain
pleasure
comfort
indignation
knowledge
Truth?

For the more
I encounter Peace
in the *panpsychic* penumbra
beyond the thresholds of mind

The more I encounter
my petty
Phaethonic projections
returning to my door
awkwardly begging
for forgiveness

The more I realize
we're refractions
seeking the Unseekable

That abiding counsel
Siduri gifted to *Gilgamesh:*

Life's a great love affair
to be devoured boldly

And
Peace
we each
carry
within

We Fear the Mystery

We are starved
for authentic connection

Starved
for a connection
with the Mystery of Life

Where once
there was awe
wonderment
trepidation
of Nature's sheer majesty
there's now a scarcely definable
infoxication

We've fragmented
our Universe
into every category
imaginable

Forgotten the sacred
lies in the inane

Lost ourselves
in syntax
and the linguistic domain

Created divisions in Reality
resembling library catalogs

Forfeited our power
to the sociopathic charlatans
of *rotting empires*

How beautiful it would be
to see Existence
as pure potentiality
rather than the lifeless
absurdly empirical definitions
we've ascribed to it

The eternal *Neti Neti*
that cannot be
grasped
named
explained
only *felt*

Whatever amazement
we feel toward Life
is swiftly stomped out of us
during childhood
and we reach adolescence
herded
by a society
disinterested in *play*

A world
estranged
by the mythos
of separation

A world where fairy tales
and the profound mythologies
of our animist Ancestors
are condescendingly denoted
as *primitive* fictions

Fit for children
but beneath the rational adult

Where's our *respect*
for Reality's vastness?

Our connection
to the effulgently existential?

Our daring to face the ethereal
free from culture's buffer?

Why do we contentedly
accept the doctrines
shoveled down our throats
from fanatical religious
political and socioeconomic
institutions?

Why do we kill
for divisive ideologies
robbing us of dignity?

How dare we claim to *know* the Truth
and wield it over others

One conscious moment
contemplating the night sky
should be enough to question
the meaning of our lives

Enough to obliterate
the delusional
self-importance
we all so dearly cling to

Enough to see
we're all connected
in an inextricable Vortex
so Intelligent
our achievements resemble
sandpit babbling

We're a part of something
so mind-boggling
that we should treat the Earth
with the reverence
a newborn
shows its Mother

Our nescience
of Nature's startling beauty
reflects contempt
for the Feminine
and a loathing of Life

Our fear of the Mystery

Who Are You?

What belongs to you?

Your house
car
land
partner
children
money
name
body
thoughts?

Perhaps
inquiring sincerely
you'll find
everything you thought
was *yours*
is a gift

And you're
a *visitor* here

Responsible
for caring gracefully
for your treasures
yet returning them
as *Solomon*
shed
his *Seal*

Because grasping this Truth
requires recognition
of what *you* really are

Where's the *I* you speak of?
This mysterious conductor
of an evanescent journey

And now
what seemed
a child's game
has morphed into
something *torturous*

Because the *I*
bandied around so definitively
can't be found
through the *senses*
nor do words
hasten an Awakening

Yet
you can feel your Essence
your *footprints*
in stillness

A sunset
silence
a moving artwork
in *Al-'Ishq Al-Ilahi*
if you allow it

For
the rabbit hole
only unfolds
when we're willing to accept
that the evidence
of our *Being*
the red herrings
aren't the *I* itself

Just as words
aren't the objects and phenomena
they describe
merely *symbols*

And that the *things*
defining us
were only projections
manifestations
traces in Time's
ever-shifting dunes

But we fighters
of Life's natural flow
are adamant
possessions and experiences
form our identity

That this world
of shaky forms
gives our *I*
its *I-ness*

For we aren't
our bodies
our *social identities*
any more than actors
are their characters

We're the substratic observers
the changeless *Ātman*
patiently coaxing
the comic tragedies
of Existence
into Oblivion
yet untainted
by the apparent actuality
of the mirage

Because
You
remains
when everything
that's seemingly yours
melts away
like snow
on a sun-soaked
footpath

We shouldn't strive
to capture this Enigma
labeling its qualities
like an exotic
zoo animal

Just realize
You are
neither external
nor internal
        but *beyond*
these monumental
guardians

Let Go

Life is suffering

The pervasive
religiophilosophical
doctrine
of the ages

Both the king
and the beggar
are in the process
of decay and return
to that *Elysian* Source
even the *rishis*
were condemned to cloak
in metaphor

Yet this ugly burden
alchemizes
when we succumb
to temporailty's
tormenting trance
by forsaking dependence
on controlling
an inherently elusive Phenomenon
and forgiving our bumbling attempts
to clutch at the phantoms of desire
realizing
the transience
of all passing before us

We don't need to *become* anything!

Becoming perpetuates
Shahrazad's
bewitching blaze

Because
Reality transcends
deities
difficult postures
austerities
mantras
or mind-bending *Somas*

Life's mysteries
surround us

Childbirth
sacred geometry
plant medicine
the power of *thought*

Realizing
the profundity
between breaths
the *Grace*
in each moment
we encounter
what we've been
awkwardly striving for
externally

That unwavering
indestructible *Logos*
silently waiting
for the *Prodigal Son*
to return
empty-handed
from the
long
   journey
      in
   the
      wilderness

Staring Back at You

And all the people you knew
in those mad streets
in the sheets

Out there between dreams
Hurled from the loves and losses
of their lives
by Forces that laughed
at their certainties

Our certainty

All those souls you knew
in this convoluted fiesta
of mind and desire
only felt like Life in human form
always reminding you
that boundaries guard
human temples
A human invention
The *gargoyles* of the psyche

That language
was only ever
mouth movements

An infinite binary
rising out of that
primordial *Aum*

we forget Exists
only through consensus

Collective thought forms
as arbitrary
as the *Gregorian Calendar*
or the color
of someone's skin

That there's a Grid
beyond causation

The *Wahdat al-Wujud*
beyond the *sub-atomic*

A luminous
interconnectedness
between all Life
as Indigenous cultures
understood *a priori*

An undying
pulsing rhythm
indifferent
to class structures
or sexual preferences

And you found
normals
between the endless arms
of lovers

rights and wrongs
under the clouds of countless cities
that you sheepishly realized
judgment
was a carefully decorated
self-imposed prison
seducing even the brightest minds
when they forgot
perspective was a *jackal*
transfigured in stolen moments
to those curious enough
to accept their own
absurdity

And the people you knew
inspired you
humbled you
created both
agony and ecstasy
between your mornings

Yet
in the wake
of each goodbye
you only ever found
your own
contradictions
staring back at you

Your Own Wheel of Life

Be your *own* wheel of Life
in a society
blinded by the lies
of *Māra's* minions

Pursue Truth
through your *own* constructs
not the perverted
credentials and creeds
strangling our Life force
in the name of
veracity

Feel each person
as *somebody's child*
hurting
hoping
praying
for change

God
masquerading
as a momentary dreamer

Live freely
honoring
the intrinsic freedom
and equality
of *all beings*

Recognizing each Life
as infinitely complex

That *sonder*
denigrated and defamed
by judgment and schisms

See *only human*
in an inhumane world

Discern *deception*
regardless
of how beautifully
it's packaged
choosing dignity
over a reductive system
spurning people as utilities
and selling them
their birthright

Respect
the sanctity of Life
wherever it manifests
remaining curious
about the Supernal
as mind and matter
divorce

You decide
where to place energy
not the psychopathic corporations

poisoning our values
and polluting our cities
with false paradigms
of beauty and happiness

Prevaricator politicians
producing *nothing*
demanding permissions
to produce

Old mahogany-marinated men
in beautiful Italian suits
who'd soil themselves
at the end of a rifle
condemning boys
to murder
their brothers

Choose art
curious minds
a frenzied celebration
of mortality

Don't be *told*
who to marry
love
trust
respect
pray to
hate

Don't be *told*
what to read
ingest
or how to expand
your Consciousness

Sedated and drip-fed
conveniently mind-altering substances
keeping industry churning
but denying expansion
and insight

Feel the undulations
of *living*
free from censor
enjoying pleasure
without the guilt
scapegoated by religion
across the millennia

Choose Peace
in a world
groaning
with cruelty

Trusting in Life
your Intuition
the Intelligence
twining the Cosmos
and in the kindness
of strangers

Trusting Love's
the inherent nature
of *Being*

Anger's
a manifestation of pain

And *fear*
hardens most hearts
not evil

Remember:

Even if the powerful
remain hollow
there are *good people*
everywhere
compassionate people
spreading *Dharma*

That wherever
you lay your head
people crave the same tenets

Seek beauty
regardless
of what's espoused by the media
regurgitated across the table
or plastered around the city walls

Be your own wheel of Life

All You Don't Know

And now you're here
in this moment
and all that matters
is how you *live it*

How humbly
you've grasped ambiguity
and who you *are*
as you let the magic *manifold*
of memory
of all you once were
melt around you

Has pain wizened you?
Mistakes bestowed gentleness?
A lack of assumptions
about morality
luck and misfortune
as you've watched all the good
arrive disguised at your feet?

Do you feel compassion
for all mortals
waking to the same
curious delusion?

Have you submitted clumsily
to your fallibly
hypocrisy

watching your edges
edge into themselves?

Has Life softened you?
Each betrayal
sweetened the beautiful moments
or calloused the corners
of your experience?

What's Love taught you
about beauty and ugliness?

That all things
are done for Love
in the name of Love
or a desperate desire
to *receive it*

And when each love ends
are you trusting
you'll love again?

That Love's
a *state of Being*

The word with a thousand faces
binding the galaxies
and dreaming the forests

Does music heal your misery?
Have the years revealed your Essence?

Has Change
unveiled Herself to be
the one *immutable law*
of the Universe?

How have you
observed *Khaos*
presiding over Life
as She observes you
frantically polarizing moments
oblivious to the words
falling off the page
and into the
somnolent limbo
between memory
and anticipation?

Do you run
from the Unknown
or race toward it?

Don't tell me
all you've learned
from Life

Tell me
all you've come to realize
you don't know!

Glossary

*

A

Abraxas (Ἀβραξας): A mystical figure in *Gnosticism*, often depicted as a deity or magical entity embodying good and evil, representing the union of opposites, and associated with the cosmos and the divine source of creation. Further reading: *"The Gnostic Religion,"* by Hans Jonas; *"The Red Book: Liber Novus,"* by Carl Gustav Jung; *"Demian,"* by Herman Hesse.

Adhan (أذان): The Islamic call to prayer traditionally recited from a mosque's minaret by a *muezzin* throughout the day. Further Reading: *"Sahih al-Bukhari,"* translated and edited by Muhammad Muhsin Khan; *"The Heart of Islam: Enduring Values for Humanity,"* by Karen Armstrong.

Aesop (Αἴσωπος/Aisōpos): A legendary ancient Greek fabulist and storyteller believed to have lived around 620–564 BCE. *Aesop* is credited with composing many fables, often featuring animals with human characteristics. Further reading: *"The Fables of Aesop,"* translated by William Caxton, edited by Joseph Jacobs.

Agape (ἀγάπη): A Greek term for "unconditional, divine love," representing a profound affection transcending physical or emotional attachment and embodying compassion and altruism. Further reading: *"The Four Loves,"* by C. S. Lewis.

AI (Artificial Intelligence): The simulation of human intelligence processes by machines, especially computer systems. These processes include learning, reasoning, and self-correction. Further Reading: *"Deep Learning,"* by Ian Goodfellow, Yoshua Bengio, and Aaron Courville.

Akashic (आकाशिक): From the Sanskrit word *ākāśa* (आकाश), meaning "ether" or "sky." In spiritual and metaphysical traditions, it refers to the *Akashic Records*, which are believed to be a compendium of all universal knowledge, events, thoughts, and experiences existing in a metaphysical or etheric plane. Further reading: *"The Akashic Records: Sacred Exploration of Your Soul's Journey Within the Wisdom of the Collective Consciousness,"* by Ernesto Ortiz.

Allah (الله): Arabic for "God" in Islam, symbolizing the singular, omnipotent deity central to Islamic faith and practice, emphasizing monotheism and the omnipotence of the divine. Further reading: *"The Quran,"* translated by Abdullah Yusuf Ali.

Aletheia (ἀλήθεια): An Ancient Greek word meaning "truth" or "disclosure." In philosophy, it refers to the state of not being hidden or the reality of things as they are, contrasting with deception or falsehood. Further reading: *"The Republic of Plato,"* by Plato, translated by Benjamin Jowett.

Al-'Ishq Al-Ilahi (العشق الإلهي): Arabic for "Divine Love," the supreme love of God. It is a profound, transcendent affection for the divine, often explored in *Sufi* poetry and philosophy as a path toward spiritual union and enlightenment. Further reading: *"The Masnavi of Rumi,"* by Jalal al-Din Rumi, translated by Jawid Mojaddedi; *"The Essential Rumi,"* by Jalal al-Din Rumi, translated by Coleman Barks.

Amba (अम्बा): *Amba* refers to a goddess in Hindu mythology often associated with *Shakti,* the divine feminine energy, as well as with power and motherhood. She is sometimes considered an aspect or form of *Parvati* (the consort of *Lord Shiva*) or *Durga* (the warrior goddess). *Amba* also means "mother" in Sanskrit. Further reading: *"The Devi Bhagavata Purana,"* by Vyasa, translated by Swami Vijnanananda.

Ambrosia (ἀμβροσία): Roughly translating to "immortality" or "immortal substance," *ambrosia* is the divine food or drink of the gods in Greek mythology. Consuming ambrosia is believed to bestow eternal youth or immortality. Further reading: *"Theogony and Works and Days,"* by Hesiod, translated by M. L. West.

Ankh (☥): An ancient Egyptian symbol representing the "Key of Life," the eternal, cyclical nature of time and immortality. It is associated with the divine and is often depicted as a cross with a loop at the top. Further reading: *"The Egyptian Book of the Dead: The Book of Going Forth by Day,"* translated by Raymond Faulkner and Ogden Goelet.

A priori: Knowledge independent of experience and derived from reason alone, considered universally true and self-evident. It contrasts with *a posteriori* knowledge, dependent on empirical evidence and experience. Further reading: *"Critique of Pure Reason,"* by Immanuel Kant, translated by Marcus Weigelt and Max Muller.

Arjuna (अर्जुन): A pivotal character in the *Mahabharata,* one of the great *Sanskrit* epics of ancient India. *Arjuna* is a renowned warrior prince from the royal *Pandava* family, one of the two factions involved in the epic's central conflict. He has a central role in the *Bhagavad Gita,* where he engages in a philosophical dialogue with *Krishna* on duty, morality, and spirituality. Further reading: *"The Bhagavad Gita: A New Translation,"* translated by Stephen Mitchell.

Ātman (आत्मा): The "true self" or "soul" in Hindu philosophy, which is considered eternal and unchanging. It is the essence connecting one to *Brahman*, the ultimate reality or universal consciousness, signifying the unity of existence. Further reading: *"The Upanishads: A New Translation,"* by Eknath Easwaran.

Aum (ॐ): A sacred syllable in Hinduism, Buddhism, and Jainism, symbolizing the essence of the universe and the ultimate reality. It represents the interconnectedness of existence and is often chanted during meditation and spiritual practices to invoke peace and unity. Further reading: *"The Mandukya Upanishad,"* translated by Swami Krishnananda.

Avidyā (अवविद्या): In Sanskrit, *avidyā* means "ignorance" or "misunderstanding," referring to the lack of true knowledge about the nature of reality. In both Hinduism and Buddhism, it is considered the root cause of human suffering, trapping individuals in the cycle of *saṃsāra* (संसार), which requires transcension for spiritual liberation. Further reading: *"Light on the Yoga Sutras of Patanjali,"* by B. K. S. Iyengar.

Ayn al-Qalb (عين القلب): Arabic for "Eye of the Heart," symbolizing inner vision or spiritual insight transcending ordinary perception, often associated with deeper understanding and awareness in mystical traditions. Further reading: *"The Meccan Revelations" (Al-Futuhat al-Makkiyya),* by Ibn Arabi, translated by William C. Chittick and James W. Morris, edited by Michel Chodkiewicz.

B

Banshee (Bean sídhe): A female spirit from Irish folklore whose haunting wail is said to foretell a family member's imminent death. Traditionally believed to be a supernatural messenger from the Otherworld. Further reading: *"Visions and Beliefs in the West of Ireland,"* by Lady Augusta Gregory and W. B Yeats.

Barabbas (אבא רב): A New Testament figure who was a prisoner chosen by the crowd to be released instead of *Jesus Christ* before *Passover,* following the tradition where the Roman governor would release one prisoner selected by the people. Further reading: *"The Bible (The New Testament): Authorized King James Version,"* by Oxford University Press.

Biophilic (biophilia): Relating to *biophilia,* the human affinity for nature. It encompasses emotional connections to living systems, promoting well-being and belonging. Further reading: *"Biophilia,"* by Edward O. Wilson; *"The Science Delusion: Freeing the Spirit of Inquiry,"* by Rupert Sheldrake.

Bodhi (बोधि): Sanskrit for "enlightenment" or "awakening" in Buddhism. It often refers to *Buddha's* enlightenment under the Bodhi tree in *Bodh Gaya,* India, and the concept of awakening in Buddhism. Further reading: *"The Dhammapada,"* by Gautama Buddha, translated by Eknath Easwaran.

Brahman (ब्रह्मा): In Hindu philosophy, *Brahman* refers to the ultimate, formless reality transcending duality and distinction. It represents universal consciousness, embodying the essence of everything in existence. In contrast to *Ātman,* which denotes the individual soul, *Brahman* is the source from which all beings arise and return. Further reading: *"The Bhagavad Gita,"* translated by Eknath Easwaran.

Brane (Membrane): A fundamental concept in *string theory*, representing a multi-dimensional object that can exist within a higher-dimensional space, where our universe may be a three-dimensional brane. *Branes* can interact and influence the dynamics of the universe, suggesting that different physical laws might apply to various branes. Further reading: *"Parallel Worlds: A Journey Through Creation, Higher Dimensions, and the Future of the Cosmos,"* by Michio Kaku.

Buddha (बुद्ध): Meaning "The Awakened One," this title refers to *Siddhartha Gautama* (c. 563–483 BCE), an Indian prince from *Lumbini* (modern-day Nepal) who, after renouncing royal life, attained enlightenment under the *Bodhi Tree* in *Bodh Gaya, India.* His teachings, including the *Four Noble Truths* and the *Eightfold Path,* form the foundation of Buddhism, guiding followers toward transcending suffering and achieving spiritual liberation. In Hinduism, the Buddha is considered the 9th avatar of *Vishnu.* Further reading: *"Buddha,"* by Karen Armstrong; *"The Dhammapada,"* translated by Eknath Easwaran; *"The Heart of the Buddha's Teaching,"* by Thich Nhat Hanh.

Burning Bush (אֲרוֹב הָנָס): A biblical narrative in which God communicates with *Moses* from a bush that is engulfed in flames but remains unconsumed. The story emphasizes revelation, transformation, and the intersection of the divine with the mortal world. Further reading: *"The Holy Scriptures: According to the Masoretic Text,"* by the Jewish Publication Society of America (Tanakh); *"The Bible (The book of Exodus 3:1-6): The Authorized King James Version,"* by Oxford University Press.

Burqa (برقع): A full-body garment worn by some Muslim women, characterized by a mesh screen covering the face and a loose-fitting design covering the entire body. In Arabic, the term can also refer to garments covering the face and body. It is often associated with cultural practices and interpretations of modesty in various Islamic traditions. Further Reading: *"Women and Gender in Islam: Historical Roots of a Modern Debate,"* by Leila Ahmed.

C

Calculus: A fundamental branch of mathematics studying continuous change. It is typically divided into two main subfields: *differential calculus,* which examines the rates at which quantities change, and *integral calculus,* which deals with the accumulation of quantities. These tools help in understanding motion, growth, and decay in both the natural and physical sciences. Further reading: *"The Mathematical Principles of Natural Philosophy,"* by Isaac Newton, translated by Charles Leedham-Green; *"The Mind of God,"* by Paul Davies.

Canaan (כְּנַעַן): An ancient region in the Near East, mentioned in biblical texts as the land promised to *Abraham's* descendants in the Bible. Source: *"The Bible (The Old Testament): The Authorized King James Version,"* by Oxford University Press.

Cartesian: Refers to the philosophy and ideas of *René Descartes,* a 17th-century French philosopher, mathematician, and scientist. Central to *Cartesian philosophy* is the method of systematic doubt and the quest for certainty. It emphasizes reason as the primary source of knowledge, contrasting with truth derived from sensory experience. Further reading: *"Meditations on First Philosophy,"* by René Descartes, translated by John Cottingham.

Charon (Χάρων): The ferryman of the dead in Greek mythology, who transports the souls of the deceased across the *River Styx* to the realm of the dead. Further reading: *"The Argonautika: The Story of Jason and the Quest for the Golden Fleece,"* by Apollonius of Rhodes, translated by Peter Green.

Chitta (चतित): Sanskrit for "mind-stuff" or "consciousness." It is the fundamental substance of the mind including the totality of cognitive processes, encompassing the individual mind in addition to the universal or collective consciousness. In Indian philosophy, *Chitta* is the repository of all mental impressions *(samskaras)* and tendencies *(vasanas).* Further reading: *"The Yoga Sutras of Patanjali,"* by Patanjali, translated by Edwin F. Bryant.

Christian Science: A religious movement founded by *Mary Baker Eddy* in the 19th century, emphasizing spiritual healing and the metaphysical interpretation of the Bible. Further Reading: *"Science and Health with Key to the Scriptures,"* by Mary Baker Eddy.

Chrysanthemum (菊花): A genus of flowering plants known for its decorative and symbolic value, especially in East Asian cultures where it represents autumn, endurance, and longevity. Further reading: *"The Chrysanthemum and the Sword: Patterns of Japanese Culture,"* by Ruth Benedict.

Cymatic/cymatics: The study of wave phenomena, exploring the relationship between sound and matter, demonstrating how vibrations influence the arrangement and behavior of physical substances. Further reading: *"Cymatics: A Study of Wave Phenomena and Vibration,"* by Hans Jenny; *"Healing Sounds: The Power of Harmonics,"* by Johnathan Goldman; *"The Hidden Life of Water,"* by Masaru Emoto.

D

Da Vinci: Refers to *Leonardo da Vinci* (1452–1519), a famous Italian Renaissance artist, scientist, and polymath revered for his contributions to art, science, and invention. Da Vinci's prolific notebooks reveal his profound explorations in integrating art and science. Further reading: *"The Notebooks of Leonardo da Vinci,"* by Leonardo de Vinci, translated by Jean Paul Richter.

Delphic (Δελφικός): Refers to the *Oracle of Delphi*, one of the most revered religious institutions in ancient Greece, located at the sanctuary of *Apollo* at *Delphi*. The oracle, often referred to as the *Pythia*, was a high priestess who served as the mouthpiece of the god *Apollo*. She delivered cryptic prophecies and guidance to individuals and city-states alike. Further reading: *"The Golden Bough: A Study in Magic and Religion,"* by James Frazer.

Dervish (درویش): Derives from the Persian "درویش" *(darvīsh)*, meaning "poor," "seeker," or "beggar." A *dervish* is a member of a *Sufi* Muslim order who takes vows of poverty and austerity, practicing mystical dancing, chanting, among other devotions to achieve spiritual ecstasy and divine union. Further reading: *"The Masnavi (Oxford World's Classics),"* by Jalal al-Din Muhammad Rumi, translated by Jawid Mojaddedi.

Dharma (धर्म): *Dharma* represents cosmic order, moral law, and ethical duty. In Hinduism, it relates to individual responsibilities based on age, caste, and gender, guiding actions in universal harmony. In Buddhism, it encompasses the *Buddha's* teachings and the path to enlightenment, focusing on ethical conduct and mental discipline. Further reading: *"The Ramayana: A Shortened Modern Prose Version of* *the Indian Epic,"* by R. K. Narayan; *"What the Buddha Taught,"* by Walpola Rahula.

Dionysian (Διονυσιακός): Referring to *Dionysus*, the Greek god of wine, fertility, and revelry. Symbolizes ecstasy, chaos, passion, and primal aspects of human nature. Further reading: *"The Birth of Tragedy,"* by Friedrich Nietzsche.

Djinn (جن): Supernatural beings in Islamic and pre-Islamic Arabian folklore, often considered to be powerful spirits able to influence the human world. Further reading: *"The Arabian Nights: Tales of 1,001 Nights,"* translated by Malcom C. Lyons and Ursula Lyons.

Dreamtime (Tjukurrpa): *Tjukurrpa* refers to a sacred era in *Australian Aboriginal* mythology during which ancestral spirits created the world. In this timeless realm, shamans can access profound spiritual knowledge. Among various Aboriginal languages, *Tjukurrpa* specifically comes from the Western Desert language group. Further reading: *"The Dreaming & Other Essays,"* by W. E. H. Stanner.

Drishti (दृष्टी): In Sanskrit, *drishti* refers to "sight" or "vision," often used in spiritual contexts to signify perception, awareness, and the ability to see beyond the physical realm. It also describes a focused gaze or vision in yoga. Further reading: *"Light on Yoga,"* by B. K. S. Iyengar.

Duende: A Spanish term for intense emotion and artistic inspiration, often associated with the spirit of creativity and the intensity of artistic expression, particularly in *flamenco* music and dance. Further reading: *"Finding Duende,"* by Federico García Lorca, translated by Christopher Maurer.

Dukkha (दुःख): In Buddhism, *dukkha* refers to the inherent suffering of life, emphasizing transcension through spiritual awakening. Further reading: *"The Four Noble Truths,"* by Geshe Tashi Tsering.

Dunya (الدنيا): Arabic for "the temporal world," representing the transience of material existence in Islamic teachings. In Islamic terminology, *Dunya* is contrasted with the eternal afterlife (الآخرة, *akhira*). It encompasses all worldly experiences and possessions, emphasizing life's transience. Further reading: *"The Quran,"* translated by Abdullah Yusuf Ali.

E

Eden (עֵדֶן): Often referred to as the *Garden of Eden,* it is a biblical paradise described in the *Book of Genesis* as humanity's original home where *Adam* and *Eve* lived before the Fall. It symbolizes innocence, abundance, and divine presence, representing an ideal state of harmony between God and creation. Further reading: *"The Bible (Book of Genesis): Authorized King James Version,"* by Oxford University Press.

Eleusinian (Ἐλευσίνιος): Refers to the *Eleusinian Mysteries,* ancient Greek religious rites held at *Eleusis.* These were secretive religious rites associated with *Demeter* and *Persephone,* focusing on death and rebirth, fertility, and the afterlife. Further reading: *"The Homeric Hymn to Demeter,"* attributed to Homer, in *"The Homeric Hymns,"* translated by Sarah Ruden; *"The Archaic Revival,"* by Terrence McKenna.

Elysian (Ἠλύσιον): Pertaining to *Elysium,* a paradisiacal realm in Greek mythology where the souls of the heroic and virtuous exist after death. Further reading: *"The Iliad,"* by Homer, translated by Robert Fagles.

Ensō (円相): A circular symbol in *Zen Buddhism* representing enlightenment, the universe, and life's interconnectedness. Typically drawn in a single stroke, it embodies the beauty of imperfection and the creative process, symbolizing both emptiness and fullness. Further reading: *"Zen Mind, Beginner's Mind,"* by Shunryu Suzuki.

Entropy (Entropie): A core concept in *thermodynamics* and *statistical mechanics, entropy* measures disorder or randomness in a system. Linked to the *second law of thermodynamics,* it states that in isolated systems, entropy increases over time, indicating that natural processes tend toward greater disorder and equilibrium. Further reading: *"The 2nd Law: Energy, Chaos, and Form,"* by P. W. Atkins; *"The Order of Time,"* by Carlo Rovelli.

Etz Chaim (עֵץ חַיִּים): Hebrew for "Tree of Life," representing divine energy and life's interconnectedness in *Kabbalistic* thought. It is a metaphor for spiritual growth and the path to enlightenment, representing the *ten sefirot,* or *emanations,* through which the divine manifests in the world. Further reading: *"The Kabbalistic Tree of Life,"* by Z'ev ben Shimon Halevi.

Excalibur: In *Arthurian* mythology, *Excalibur* is *King Arthur's* legendary sword, famously embedded in a stone, which only he could pull out, signifying his rightful sovereignty over Britain. Often associated with magical properties, Excalibur symbolizes divine kingship and the qualities of true leadership. Further reading: *"Le Morte D'Arthur: King Arthur and the Legends of the Round Table,"* by Sir Thomas Malory, translated by Keith Baines.

210

Ex nihilo *(ex nihilo)*: Latin for "out of nothing," used in philosophical and theological contexts to describe the creation of the universe by divine will or power without any pre-existing material. It emphasizes creation as uniquely generating existence from non-existence. Further reading: *"Summa Theologica,"* by St. Thomas Aquinas, translated by The Fathers of the English Dominican Province.

F

Faust: A character in German legend, famously portrayed by *Goethe*, who makes a pact with the Devil for worldly knowledge and pleasure. Further reading: *"Faust,"* by Johann Wolfgang von Goethe, translated by Walter Kaufmann.

Flavian (Flavius): *Flavian* generally refers to the *Flavian* dynasty, a Roman imperial family that ruled from 69 AD to 96 AD. The Flavian emperors are known for commissioning the *Colosseum* in Rome. Further reading: *"The Twelve Caesars,"* by Suetonius, translated by Robert Graves; *"SPQR: A History of Ancient Rome,"* by Mary Beard.

Flower of Life: The *Flower of Life* represents the cycle of creation and the interconnectedness of all living things. It symbolizes harmony, unity, and the universal blueprint. Further reading: *"The Ancient Secret of the Flower of Life,"* by Drunvalo Melchizedek; *"Sacred Geometry: Philosophy & Practice (Art and Imagination),"* by Robert Lawlor.

Fool's Journey: A metaphorical narrative in *tarot* depicting the spiritual and personal development of an individual through the *Major Arcana* cards. It represents the stages of life, growth, and self-discovery as the Fool encounters various archetypes and experiences. Further reading: *"The Pictorial*

Key to the Tarot," by Arthur Edward Waite; *"The Tarot: History, Symbolism, and Divination,"* by Robert Place.

Fountain of Youth (Fuente de la Juventud): A legendary cross-cultural myth of a spring restoring the youth of anyone who drinks or bathes in its waters. The search for the Fountain of Youth is primarily attributed to Spanish explorer *Juan Ponce de León*. Further reading: *"The Travels of Sir John Mandeville,"* by John Mandeville, translated by Charles Moseley; *"The Greek Alexander Romance,"* translated by Richard Stoneman; *"The Florida of the Inca,"* by Garcilaso de la Vega, translated by John Grier Varner and Jeannette Varner.

G

Gaia (Γαῖα): In Greek Mythology, *Gaia* personifies the Earth and the primordial goddess from whom all life originates. She is often revered as a nurturing mother figure associated with fertility, the natural world, and life's interconnectedness. Further reading: *"The Orphic Hymns,"* translated by Apostolos N. Athanassakis and Benjamin M. Wolkow.

Galahad: A knight of the *Round Table* in *Arthurian legend*, renowned for his purity, virtue, chivalry, and his quest for, and discovery of, the *Holy Grail*. Further reading: *"Le Morte D'Arthur: King Arthur and the Legends of the Round Table,"* by Sir Thomas Malory, translated by Keith Baines; *"The Power of Myth,"* by Joseph Campbell.

Ganges (गंगा): A sacred river in India, revered in Hinduism as a personification of the goddess *Ganga*. It is considered a source of spiritual purity and is the site of religious rituals, pilgrimages, and ceremonies. Further reading: *"Ganges: The Many Pasts of an Indian River,"* by Sudipta Sen.

Gargoyles (Gargouille): Architectural features used in *Gothic architecture,* often in the form of grotesque figures or creatures. *Gargoyles* are known for their distinct, frightening appearances. Further reading: *"The Gargoyles of Notre-Dame: Medievalism and the Monsters of Modernity,"* by Michael Camille.

Genghis Khan (成吉思汗): The founder and first *Great Khan* of the *Mongol Empire,* uniting the Mongol tribes and expanding his territory across Asia and into Europe during the early 13th century. He established one of the largest contiguous empires in history, significantly influencing trade and cultural exchange along the *Silk Road.* His conquests involved extreme brutality, including widespread massacres and the destruction of entire cities. Further reading: *"Genghis Khan and the Making of the Modern World,"* by Jack Weatherford.

Ghumūḍ al-ḥayāh (غموض الحياة): Arabic for "the mirage of life" or "the obscuring of life." It symbolizes the illusory nature of existence, suggesting that life can be perceived as a dream or mirage. Further reading: *"The Sufi Path of Knowledge: Ibn al-Arabi's Metaphysics of Imagination,"* by William C. Chittick.

Gilgamesh (𒄑𒂆𒈦): *Gilgamesh* is a legendary king of *Uruk,* featured in ancient *Mesopotamian* literature, particularly the *Epic of Gilgamesh,* one of the earliest known works of literary fiction. He is portrayed as both human and divine, embodying the themes of friendship, heroism, and the quest for immortality. The epic is considered a cross-cultural blueprint, establishing narrative arcs and themes that resonate throughout subsequent literature, including the story of *Noah's Ark* and many other mythologies. Further reading: *"The Epic of Gilgamesh,"* translated by Andrew George.

Giza (الجيزة): A plateau located near modern *Cairo, Egypt,* home to the Great Pyramids of *Khufu, Khafre,* and *Menkaure,* and the Great *Sphinx.* These monuments remain mysteries and are among the Seven Wonders of the Ancient World and symbolize the pinnacle of ancient Egyptian thought. Further Reading: *"Fingerprints of the Gods: The Evidence of Earth's Lost Civilization,"* by Graham Hancock; *"The Orion Mystery: Unlocking the Secrets of the Pyramids,"* by Robert Bauval and Adrian Gilbert; *"Serpent in the Sky: The High Wisdom of Ancient Egypt,"* by John Anthony West.

Gnosis (γνῶσις): Originates from the Greek word for "knowledge" and refers to spiritual insight transcending ordinary understanding, particularly in *Gnostic* and early Christian contexts. It emphasizes personal spiritual experience and realization of divine truths, contrasting material existence with a higher spiritual reality, as reflected in Gnostic texts like the *Gospel of Thomas* and the *Gospel of Truth.* Further reading: *"Nag Hammadi Library,"* by James M. Robinson.

Gomorrah (עֲמֹרָה): One of the two biblical cities, alongside *Sodom,* destroyed by divine judgment due to their wickedness and immorality. Often associated with sin and vice, *Gomorrah* symbolizes moral degradation in religious texts. Further reading: *"The Bible (The Book of Genesis): Authorized King James Version,"* by Oxford University Press.

Grail (Graal): Refers to *The Holy Grail,* a legendary object in medieval literature, primarily associated with Christian mythology and *Arthurian legend.* It is typically depicted as a chalice or cup possessing miraculous powers, such as providing eternal youth. Further reading: *"The Arthurian Romances,"* by Chrétien de Troyes, translated by William Kibler; *"The Hero with a Thousand Faces,"* by Joseph Campbell.

214

Gregorian Calendar (Calendarium Gregorianum): The calendar system used by most of the world today, introduced by *Pope Gregory XIII* in 1582 to reform the *Julian calendar.* Further reading: *"The Calendar: The 5000-year Struggle to Align the Clock and the Heavens—and What Happened to the Missing Ten Days,"* by David Ewing Duncan.

H

Hades (Ἄδης): The Greek god of the underworld and the ruler of the dead. *Hades* also refers to the underworld, a realm where souls go after death. Further reading: *"The Odyssey,"* by Homer, translated by Robert Fagles.

Hail Mary: A traditional Catholic prayer requesting the intercession of the *Virgin Mary,* the mother of *Jesus.* It highlights themes of grace, mercy, and spiritual support for believers. Further reading: *"The Secret of the Rosary,"* by St. Louis de Montfort.

Hajj (ﺣﺞ): The mandatory Islamic pilgrimage to *Mecca,* performed by Muslims who are physically and financially able at least once in their lifetime. Occurring in the month of *Dhu al-Hijjah,* it includes essential rituals commemorating the actions of the *Prophet Ibrahim (Abraham)* and his family. Further reading: *"The Quran,"* translated by Abdullah Yusuf Ali.

Hare Krishna (हरि कृष्ण): A mantra associated with followers of *Krishna Consciousness,* worshipping *Krishna.* Further reading: *"Science of Self-Realization,"* by A. C. Bhaktivedanta Swami Prabhupada.

Heka (☉◡⌐): In ancient Egyptian belief, *Heka* represents the divine power of magic crucial for creation and cosmic order. It is both a deity and the energy harnessed by gods and humans. Further reading: *"The Ancient Egyptian Coffin Texts,"* by Raymond O. Faulkner; *"Magic in Ancient Egypt: Revised Edition,"* by Geraldine Pinch.

Hell: A term derived from the Old English *hel*, referring to a concealed place associated with the dead and punishment. In biblical contexts, it encompasses various concepts represented by the Hebrew *Sheol* (the grave), the Greek *Hades* (the abode of the dead), and Hebrew *Gehenna* (a place of torment). Although the term *hell* does not appear in original biblical texts, it is synonymous with ideas of separation from God and eternal suffering in Christian theology. Further reading: *"The Bible (The Book of Revelation): The Authorized King James Version,"* by Oxford University Press.

Hemlock (Conium maculatum): A poisonous plant used in ancient executions, most notably in ancient Greece, where it was employed to execute the philosopher *Socrates*. Further reading: *"Phaedo,"* by Plato, translated by David Gallop.

Herculean (Herculeus): Relating to the mythological demigod *Hercules (Heracles/Ἡρακλῆς* in Greek mythology), renowned for his extraordinary strength and heroic feats during the *Twelve Labors.* Further reading: *"The Library (Bibliotheca),"* by Apollodorus, translated by Sir James Frazer; *"Heracles,"* by Emma Stafford.

Hermetic: Refers to the teachings and philosophical traditions attributed to *Hermes Trismegistus,* a legendary figure believed to be a fusion of the Greek god *Hermes* and the Egyptian god *Thoth. Hermeticism* encompasses various esoteric beliefs, including alchemy, astrology, and the pursuit of spiritual knowledge, emphasizing the interconnectedness of the universe and the divine. Further reading: *"Hermetica: The Greek Corpus Hermeticum and the Latin Asclepius in a New English Translation, with Notes and Introduction,"* translated by Brian P. Copenhaver.

Hierophany: Originates from the Greek words *hero* (ἥρως), meaning "hero" or "demigod," and *phanes* (φαίνω), meaning "to show" or "to reveal." It is a manifestation or revelation of the sacred or the divine. It describes moments or experiences where the sacred is revealed to individuals, often leading to profound, transformative spiritual insights. Further reading: *"The Sacred and the Profane: The Nature of Religion,"* by Mircea Eliade, translated by Willard R. Trask.

Holographic: Refers to the concept in theoretical physics known as the *holographic principle*, which posits that the universe can be seen as a two-dimensional information structure "projected" into three dimensions, implying that our perception of three-dimensional space is illusory. Further reading: *"The Holographic Universe,"* by Michael Talbot.

House of Wisdom (Bayt al-Hikma; بيت الحكمة): An academic institution and library in *Baghdad* during the *Islamic Golden Age,* established under the *Abbasid Caliphate.* It served as a major center for scientific research, scholarly activity, and translation of Greek, Persian, and Indian sources into Arabic. It was essential to the development of mathematics, astronomy, medicine, and philosophy. Further reading: *"The House of Wisdom: How Arabic Science Saved Ancient Knowledge and Gave Us the Renaissance,"* by Jim Al-Khalili.

Hydra (Ὕδρᾱ): In Greek mythology, the *Hydra* is a multi-headed serpent known for its regenerative ability; when one head is severed, two more grow back in its place. *Heracles* defeated it during one of his *twelve labors*, symbolizing the struggle against insurmountable challenges. Further reading: *"The Greek Myths: The Complete and Definitive Edition,"* by Robert Graves.

I

Icarun/Icarus (Ἴκαρος): Referring to *Icarus,* a hubristic figure from Greek mythology, known for flying too close to the sun with wings made of feathers and wax, which melted under the sun's heat, causing him to fall into the sea and drown. Further reading: *"The Metamorphoses,"* by Ovid, translated by David Raeburn.

J

Jackal (šaghāl): *Jackals* are often perceived as symbols of cunning, intelligence, and deceit in various mythologies. They are sometimes associated with death and the afterlife, as in ancient Egyptian mythology where the god *Anubis* is depicted with the head of a jackal. Further reading: *"Egyptian Mythology: A Guide to the Gods, Goddesses, and Traditions of Ancient Egypt,"* by Geraldine Pinch.

Janus (Ianus): The Roman god of beginnings, endings, and transitions, often depicted with two faces looking in opposite directions. He symbolizes the duality of time, overseeing the past and future, and is associated with gates, doorways, and portals. Further reading: *"The Romans and Their Gods,"* by R. M. Ogilvie.

Jonah (יוֹנָה): A Hebrew prophet in the Old Testament commanded by God to preach repentance to the city of *Nineveh.* After fleeing God's command and being swallowed by a great fish (often considered a whale), *Jonah* repented and fulfilled his mission. Further reading: *"The Bible (The Book of Jonah): The Authorized King James Version,"* by Oxford University Press.

Joycean: *Joycean* refers to anything related to *James Joyce,* the renowned Irish modernist writer. The word is used to describe his literary style, themes, and characteristics. Further reading: *"Ulysses"* and *"Finnegans Wake,"* by James Joyce.

K

Kalic/Kali (काली): Referring to *Kali,* the Hindu goddess of destruction, transformation, and liberation. Often depicted with a fierce appearance, she represents the divine feminine, time, change, and the cyclicality of existence. *Kali* is worshipped as a protector against evil and embodies the cycle of creation and destruction. Further reading: *"Hindu Goddesses: Visions of the Divine Feminine in the Hindu Religious Tradition,"* by David Kinsley.

Khaos (Χάος): In Greek mythology, *Khaos* (Chaos) is the personification of the primordial void or the state of the universe before the creation of the cosmos. It represents the initial gap created by the separation of heaven and earth, disorder, and the potential for the cosmos to form from nothingness. Further reading: *"The Complete World of Greek Mythology,"* by Richard Buxton; *"Chaos, Creativity, and Cosmic Consciousness,"* by Rupert Sheldrake, Ralph Abraham, and Terence McKenna.

Khayal (خیال): Arabic for "imagination" or "fantasy." In Arabic philosophy, particularly within Islamic thought, *khayal* refers to the imaginative faculty of the mind, which is essential for understanding abstractions and metaphysical realities. It is often associated with the ability to form mental images transcending ordinary perception, facilitating deeper insights into existence and the divine. Further reading: *"The Bezels of Wisdom (Fuṣūṣ al-Ḥikam),"* by Ibn al-Arabi, translated by R. W. J. Austin; *"Diwan-e-Ghalib,"* translated by Kuldip Salil.

Knossos (Κνωσός): An ancient city on *Crete*, the center of the *Minoan civilization* (2000–1400 BCE), revered for its elaborate palace and the myth of the *Minotaur. Knossos* is often associated with matriarchal culture due to the prominence of goddess worship and female leadership. Its fall marked a shift toward patriarchal societies in the ancient Mediterranean, following the *Mycenaean* conquest and natural disasters. Further reading: *"The Chalice and the Blade: Our History, Our Future,"* by Riane Eisler.

Koan (公案): A paradoxical statement or question used in *Zen Buddhism* to provoke profound thought and challenge logical reasoning. It serves as a meditative tool to aid practitioners in attaining enlightenment and transcending conventional understanding. Further reading: *"The Book of Serenity: One Hundred Zen Dialogues,"* attributed to Zhaozhou Congshen, translated by Thomas Cleary.

Krishna (कृष्ण): A major Hindu deity, known for his role in the *Bhagavad Gita. Krishna* is revered as the eighth avatar of *Vishnu* and a manifestation of *Brahman.* Further reading: *"The Mahabharata,"* translated by John D. Smith; *"The Bhagavad Gita,"* translated by Stephen Mitchell.

L

Lahzeh (لحظه): Persian for "moment" or "instant." It denotes a brief time period, emphasizing time's fleeting and transient nature. Further reading: *"The Ultimate Divan of Hafez,"* by Hafez, translated by Paul Smith.

Lao Tzu (老子): An ancient Chinese philosopher traditionally credited with authoring the *Tao Te Ching*. Believed to have lived during the 6th century BCE (potentially the 4th to 5th century BCE), *Lao Tzu* is credited as the founder of *Taoism*. His teachings emphasize the importance of harmonizing with the *Tao* (the Way), promoting simplicity, humility, and a profound understanding of nature. Further reading: *"Tao Te Ching,"* by Lao Tzu, translated by Stephen Mitchell.

Lapis lazuli (لاژورد): A deep-blue metamorphic rock used as a semi-precious stone that has been prized since antiquity for its intense color. It is composed primarily of the mineral lazurite, calcite, sodalite, and pyrite. Further reading: *"Natural History: A Selection,"* by Pliny the Elder, translated by John F. Healey.

Lethic/Lethe (Λήθη): Refers to *Lethe,* one of the five rivers of the underworld in Greek mythology. *Lethe* is the river of forgetfulness, from which souls drank to forget their earthly lives before reincarnation. Further reading: *"The Odyssey,"* by Homer, translated by Robert Fagles; *"The Aeneid,"* by Virgil, translated by Robert Fagles.

Logarithmic Helix: A spiral pattern characterized by a consistent angle of growth around a central axis, often found in nature and mathematics (e.g., galaxies and shells). In cosmic contexts, it reflects the arrangement of matter influenced by gravitational forces, particularly evident in the spiral arms of galaxies such as the *Milky Way*. Further reading: *"The Curves of Life,"* by Sir Theodore A. Cook.

Logos (λόγος): In ancient Greek philosophy, *Logos* refers to "reason," "word," or "principle," representing the rational order of the universe; later adopted in *Christian theology* to denote the divine *Word* or *Christ* as the embodiment of divine reason. Further reading: *"Heraclitus: Fragments,"* by Heraclitus, translated by Brooks Haxton.

M

Ma (間): In Japanese aesthetics, *ma* refers to negative space or the interval between elements, emphasizing the interplay between presence and absence. It encompasses both physical and metaphysical dimensions. It is essential in various art forms, where the absence of form creates meaning and enhances the experience. Further reading: *"The Book of Tea,"* by Okakura Kazuko.

Magick: A term encompassing various ancient and global practices, rituals, and beliefs aimed at influencing the spiritual and physical world through the harnessing of spiritual energies, the manipulation of symbols, rituals, and the invocation of deities or spirits to alter reality. It has been practiced in various forms across cultures, including *shamanism, alchemy, folk traditions, Wicca,* and *ceremonial magic.* Further reading: *"The Encyclopedia of Magic and Alchemy,"* by Rosemary Ellen Guiley; *"The Sacred History: How Angels, Mystics and Higher Intelligence Made Our World,"* by Jonathan Black.

Mana: In various *Pacific Island* cultures, particularly *Polynesia, mana* refers to a spiritual force or energy believed to reside in people, objects, and the environment. It is associated with power, authority, and spiritual effectiveness, often linked to the divine. Further reading: *"Patterns in Comparative Religion,"* by Mircea Eliade, translated by Rosemary Sheed.

Mandala (मण्डल): In Hinduism and Buddhism, a *mandala* is a symbolic geometric figure, typically circular, representing the universe. Found across cultures, it serves as a spiritual tool for meditation to deepen consciousness. Composed of intricate patterns and motifs, mandalas symbolize the connection between the individual and the cosmos. Further reading: *"Psychology and Alchemy,"* by Carl Gustav Jung.

Manifold: In mathematics, a *manifold* is a space locally resembling *Euclidean* space; in esoteric contexts, it represents multiple dimensions or layers of reality. Further reading: *"The Nature of Space and Time,"* by Stephen Hawking and Roger Penrose.

Mantra (मंत्र): A sacred word, sound, or phrase believed to hold spiritual power in Hinduism, Buddhism, and other traditions. Derived from two Sanskrit roots, *"man"* (मन), meaning "mind" or "to think," and *"tra"* (त्र), meaning "instrument" or "tool," a mantra is understood as an instrument of thought used to focus or liberate the mind. It is often repeated during meditation, prayer, or rituals to invoke divine blessings, create positive vibrations, and elevate consciousness. Further reading: *"The Hymns of the Rigveda,"* translated by Ralph T. H. Griffith.

Māra (मारा): In Buddhism, *Māra* is the personification of temptation and illusion, often depicted as a demon distracting individuals from achieving enlightenment. He confronted the *Buddha* as he meditated under the *Bodhi tree*, attempting to distract him from attaining enlightenment, representing the obstacles of desire and attachment hindering spiritual awakening. Further reading: *"The Miracle of Mindfulness: An Introduction to the Practice of Meditation,"* by Thich Nhat Hanh, translated by Mobi Ho.

Maya Angelou: A renowned American poet and writer. Her work focuses on themes of identity, resilience, and racial injustice, making her a lasting voice in American literature and civil rights. Further reading: *"I Know Why the Caged Bird Sings,"* by Maya Angelou.

Mayan Calendar: A complex system of interlocking cycles used by the ancient *Maya* civilization to track time, combining a 260-day ritual calendar *(Tzolk'in)* and a 365-day solar calendar *(Haab')*. *The Long Count calendar* reached the end of one major cycle on December 21, 2012. This generated global speculation, as some believed it marked the end of the world. Further Reading: *"The Ancient Maya,"* by Robert J. Sharer and Loa P. Traxler.

Mecca (مكة): A city in Saudi Arabia and the holiest site in Islam, revered as the birthplace of the *Prophet Muhammad.* It is home to the *Kaaba,* located within the *Masjid al-Haram,* where millions of Muslims perform the *Hajj* pilgrimage annually. Further reading: *"Mecca: The Sacred City,"* by Ziauddin Sardar.

Merkaba (מרכבה): A concept in Jewish mysticism, symbolizing a divine chariot or vehicle of ascension, often representing the soul's spiritual journey toward God. It is described in *Ezekiel's* visions and central to the *Merkaba* mystical tradition, which focuses on meditation and divine encounters. Further Reading: *"Major Trends in Jewish Mysticism"* and *"On the Kabbalah and Its Symbolism,"* by Gershom Scholem.

224

Monad (μονάς): In philosophical contexts, a *monad* refers to an indivisible and simple entity. It is often associated with the idea of a fundamental unit of existence, which can be a basic building block of reality in metaphysics. The concept is used to discuss the nature of substance, perception, and existence. Further reading: *"Monadology,"* by Gottfried Wilhelm Leibniz, translated by Lloyd Strickland.

Multiverse: The concept of multiple or parallel universes existing alongside ours, often discussed in theoretical physics and cosmology. The concept is discussed in models like quantum mechanics' *many-worlds interpretation* and *string theory.* Further reading: *"The Hidden Reality: Parallel Universes and the Deep Laws of the Cosmos,"* by Brian Greene.

N

Neti Neti (नेति नेति): A Sanskrit phrase meaning "not this, not this," used in *Advaita Vedanta* philosophy to denote the practice of negation to describe the ultimate reality *(Brahman)* or the nature of the self. It emphasizes the process of elimination to transcend conceptual limitations and recognize the ineffable. Further reading: *"The Upanishads: A New Translation,"* translated by Vernon Katz and Thomas Egenes.

Nirvanic/Nirvana (निर्वाण): In *Sanskrit* and *Pali, Nirvana* is a central concept in Buddhism representing liberation from the cycle of birth, death, and rebirth *(samsara).* It signifies the extinguishing of desire and suffering, leading to enlightenment. Further reading: *"The Long Discourses of the Buddha: A Translation of the Dīgha Nikāya,"* translated by Maurice Walshe.

Non-Euclidean: Any geometry not based on the axioms and postulates of *Euclidean* geometry. *Non-Euclidean* geometries describe curved surfaces, such as those in spherical or hyperbolic spaces. Further reading: *"Euclid's Elements,"* by Euclid, edited by Dana Densmore, translated by T. L. Heath; *"Euclidean and Non-Euclidean Geometries: Development and History,"* by Marvin Jay Greenberg.

O

Olympus/Olympian (Ὄλυμπος/Ὀλύμπιος): Refers to *Mount Olympus* in Greek mythology, regarded as the dwelling place of the gods, as well as the deities themselves known as the *Olympians*. This term embodies the divine authority and mythology surrounding ancient Greek religious beliefs. Further reading: *"The Iliad,"* by Homer, translated by Robert Fagles.

Omar Khayyam (عمر خیّام): A renowned Persian polymath, poet, astronomer, and mathematician (1048–1131), best known for his poetic work, *The Rubaiyat,* which explores life, fate, and the ephemerality of existence. Further reading: *"Rubaiyat of Omar Khayyam,"* by Omar Khayyam, translated by Edward Fitzgerald.

Ouroboros/Ouroboric (ὄφις ἑαυτοῦ): An ancient symbol of a serpent or dragon eating its tail, representing the cyclical nature of life, death, and rebirth. Found cross-culturally, it signifies infinity, self-sufficiency, and life's interconnectedness, often appearing in alchemical and mystical contexts. Further reading: *"The Myth of the Eternal Return: Cosmos and History,"* by Mircea Eliade, translated by Willard R. Trask.

P

Panpsychic: Derived from the Greek words *"pan" (πᾶν),* meaning "all," and *"psyche" (ψυχή),* meaning "soul" or "mind." Refers to the philosophical view that consciousness, mind, or soul is a fundamental, universally pervasive feature. In *panpsychism,* all matter possesses consciousness or mind-like qualities, suggesting that the capacity for experience or awareness exists in everything. Further reading: *"De Anima,"* by Aristotle, translated by C. D. C Reeve; *"Process and Reality,"* by Alfred North Whitehead; *"The Rebirth of Nature: The Greening of Science and God,"* by Rupert Sheldrake

Persephone (Περσεφόνη): In Greek mythology, *Persephone* is the daughter of *Zeus* and *Demeter,* and the queen of the underworld after being abducted by *Hades.* She represents the cycle of life, death, and rebirth, as her annual return from the underworld is linked to the changing seasons. Further reading: *"The Homeric Hymns,"* translated by Sarah Ruden.

Peter Pan: A fictional character known for never growing up and living in the magical realm of *Neverland.* Further reading: *"Peter Pan,"* by J. M. Barrie.

Phaetonic/Phaethon (Φαέθων): In Greek mythology, *Phaethon* was the son of *Helios,* the sun god. He famously ambitiously attempted to drive his father's sun chariot across the sky, resulting in disastrous consequences. Further reading: *"Metamorphoses,"* by Ovid, translated by David Raeburn.

Pharisees (פְּרוּשִׁים): A prominent religious group in Judaism during the *Second Temple* period, known for their strict observance of Jewish law. In the Bible, they clash with *Jesus* over interpretations of the law and religious practices, with Jesus critiquing their ethics, legalism, and hypocrisy. Further reading: *"The Bible (The New Testament) The Authorized King James Version,"* by Oxford University Press.

Photon: A basic unit of light and electromagnetic radiation, carrying energy proportional to its frequency. It has no mass at rest, enabling it to travel at the speed of light. This characteristic makes photons essential in understanding *quantum physics* and *optics.* Further reading: *"The Collected Papers of Albert Einstein,"* by Albert Einstein, translated by Anna Beck.

Plato (Πλάτων): An ancient Greek philosopher and student of *Socrates, Plato* is renowned for his foundational contributions to Western philosophy, particularly through dialogues exploring ethics, politics, metaphysics, and epistemology. His *Theory of Forms* posits that non-material abstract forms, rather than the physical world, represent the highest level of reality. Further reading: *"Plato: Complete Works,"* edited by John M. Cooper and D. S. Hutchinson.

Prajapatic/Prajapati (पूरजापतिं): Refers to *Prajapati.* In Hindu mythology, Prajapati is considered a synonym for a creator god predating *Brahma.* The term translates to "lord of creatures," and in the *Vedic* texts, he is associated with creation and represents the primordial, universal force. Further reading: *"The Rig Veda: An Anthology,"* translated by Wendy Doniger.

Prodigal Son (ὁ ἄσωτος υἱός): The protagonist in a New Testament parable who demands his inheritance, squanders it recklessly and returns home in repentance, where his father forgives him. Further reading: *"The Bible (The Gospel of Luke) The Authorized King James Version,"* by Oxford University Press.

Q

Quantum: The smallest discrete quantity of energy or matter in *quantum mechanics.* In physics, *quantum* describes the study of physical phenomena at microscopic scales, such as *electrons* and *photons,* where energy is quantized. Further reading:*"Quantum Mechanics (The Theoretical Minimum),"* by Leonard Susskind and Art Friedman.

Quintessence (quinta essentia): The fifth element believed in ancient and medieval philosophy to be the purest essence that composes celestial bodies and the heavenly realm. In modern science, it describes a hypothetical form of dark energy responsible for the universe's accelerated expansion. Further reading: *"Metaphysics,"* by Aristotle, translated by Joe Sachs.

R

Rishis (ऋषि): Ancient sages in Hinduism revered for composing sacred texts, such as the *Vedas* and the *Upanishads,* and imparting spiritual wisdom. The *Rishis* are believed to have attained divine knowledge through deep meditation and spiritual practices, entering a heightened state of awareness that allowed them to connect with *Brahman.* Further reading: *"The Science of the Rishis,"* by Mataji Devi Vanamali; *"Wisdom of the Rishis: The Three Upanishads—Ishavasya, Kena & Mandukya,"* by Sri M; *"Vedic Yoga: The Path of the Rishi,"* by David Frawley.

Rosa Mystica: A Latin title for the *Virgin Mary* in Catholic tradition, symbolizing her purity and her role as a spiritual mother. *Rosa Mystica* translates to "Mystical Rose" and emphasizes Mary's divine grace and purity. Further reading: *"The Gospels of Mary: The Secret Tradition of Mary Magdalene,* *the Companion of Jesus,"* by Marvin Meyer; *"When God Was a Woman,"* by Merlin Stone.

Ruh (روح): In Arabic, *Ruh* translates to "spirit" or "soul" and is a central concept in Islamic theology, representing the non-material essence of a being. It is believed to be the divine breath animating life, distinguishing living beings from inanimate objects. In *Sufi* mysticism, *Ruh* signifies a deeper spiritual reality and connection to the divine, emphasizing the soul's journey toward unity with God. Further reading: *"The Study Quran,"* by Seyyed Hossein Nasr, Caner K. Dagli, Maria Massi Dakake, Joseph E.B. Lumbard, and Mohammed Rustom.

S

Sabr (صبر): Arabic for "patience" or "perseverance" in Islamic contexts. It is frequently mentioned in the *Quran* and *Hadith* literature. Further reading: *"The Alchemy of Happiness,"* by Abu Hamid Al-Ghazzali, translated by Claud Field.

Saṃsāra (संसार): In Hinduism and Buddhism, *Saṃsāra* refers to the cycle of birth, death, and rebirth, encompassing reincarnation. It represents the transience of existence, where beings are trapped in a perpetual cycle of suffering influenced by their *karma*. In these traditions, the ultimate goal is to achieve liberation *(mokṣa* or *nirvāṇa)* from *Saṃsāra,* ending the cycle and attaining enlightenment. Further reading: *"The Bhagavad Gita as It Is,"* by A. C. Bhaktivedanta Swami Prabhupada; *"The Wheel of Life: Buddhist Perspectives on Cause and Effect,"* by The Dalai Lama, translated by Jeffrey Hopkins.

Sapna (सपना): A Sanskrit and Hindi word for "dream." In philosophical contexts, *sapna* often also signifies the ephemerality of existence, highlighting the distinction between reality and illusion. Further reading: *"Mandukya Upanisad with Gaudapada's Karikaka: Truth Witness of Waking, Dream and Deep Sleep,"* by Swami Chinmayananda.

Sari (śāṭī; शाटी): *Sari* originates from the Sanskrit word *śāṭī* (शाटी), meaning "strip of cloth." The *sari* is a traditional garment worn by women in the Indian subcontinent, consisting of a long piece of cloth that is draped around the body. Further reading: *"Saris of India: Tradition and Beyond,"* by Ṛta Kapur Chishti.

Saudade (saudade): A Portuguese term for a profound emotional state of nostalgic longing for someone or something that one loves and lost, or a distant place. It captures melancholy, love, and a sense of incompleteness. *Saudade* reflects the beauty and pain of memories, often associated with longing for moments that can never be fully recaptured. Further reading: *"The Book of Disquiet,"* by Fernando Pessoa, translated by Margaret Jull Costa.

Shades (Σκιᾰς): In Greek mythology, *shades* (or shadows) refer to the souls or spirits of the dead. They inhabit the underworld, also known as *Hades,* where they exist in a shadowy, insubstantial form. Further reading: *"The Complete World of Greek Mythology,"* by Richard Buxton; *"The Divine Comedy: Inferno, Purgatorio, Paradiso,"* by Dante Alighieri, translated by Robin Kirkpatrick.

Shaktic (शक्ति): Referring to *Shakti,* the divine feminine energy in Hinduism that is the source of creation and the dynamic force of the universe. Often associated with various goddesses, Shakti embodies strength, fertility, and creativity. It is considered a cosmic energy and a personal force within individuals, representing the dance between masculine and feminine energies in spiritual and material existence. Further reading: *"Shiva Purana,"* translated by J. L. Shastri; *"Shakti: Realm of the Divine Mother,"* by Mataji Devi Vanamali.

Shaman (šaman): A spiritual practitioner found in various indigenous cultures, often acting as a healer, mediator, and guide between the physical and spiritual world. *Shamans* use rituals, trance states, and the power of natural elements to access spiritual realms for healing, divination, and guidance. Further reading: *"Shamanism: Archaic Techniques of Ecstasy,"* by Mircea Eliade, translated by Wendy Doniger; *"The Shaman: Voyages of the Soul, Trance, Ecstasy and Healing from Siberia to the Amazon,"* by Piers Vitebsky; *"The Teachings of Don Juan: A Yaqui Way of Knowledge,"* by Carlos Castaneda.

Shambhala (शम्भल/འབས་ང་འ): In Hindu and Tibetan Buddhist traditions, *Shambhala* is both a mystical, hidden kingdom believed to embody peace, enlightenment, and spiritual prosperity, and a metaphorical realm representing the pursuit of inner harmony and the awakening of collective consciousness. It is often linked with the prophesized arrival of an enlightened teacher or ruler who will guide humanity toward harmonious living. In Hinduism, Shambhala is a prophesized birthplace of *Kalki*. Further reading: *"Shambhala: The Sacred Path of the Warrior,"* by Chögyam Trungpa.

Shangri-La: A fictional, utopian paradise described in the novel *Lost Horizon*. In the story, *Shangri-La* is a mystical, isolated valley located in the Tibetan mountains. It is characterized by peace, tranquility, and an ageless, almost immortal quality among its inhabitants. Further reading: *"Lost Horizon,"* by James Hilton.

Sharazad/Scheherazade (شهرزاد): The storyteller from *One Thousand and One Nights,* who captivates *King Shahryar* with her tales to delay her execution. Further reading: *"The Arabian Nights: Tales from a Thousand and One Nights,"* translated by Richard Burton.

Shivic/Shiva (शिव): Refers to *Shiva,* a principal Hindu deity representing both destruction and creation in the cosmic cycle. As the god of transformation, he is worshipped in various forms, including the ascetic yogi and the cosmic dancer *(Nataraja),* symbolizing life's perpetual renewal. Further reading: *"Shiva: The Lord of Yoga,"* by David Frawley.

Simorgh (سیمرغ): In Persian mythology and literature, the *Simorgh* is a revered mythical bird known for its immense wisdom and healing powers. Often interpreted as a metaphor for God, it is depicted as a majestic, benevolent creature symbolizing spiritual enlightenment, the quest for knowledge, and the triumph of good over evil. Further reading: *"The Conference of the Birds (منطق‌الطیر, Mantiq al-Tayr),"* by Farid al-Din Attar, translated by Sholeh Wolpé.

Sinai (סיני): *Mount Sinai* is a mountain that is central to Judaism, Christianity, and Islam. It is considered the site where *Moses* received the Ten Commandments from God. Further reading: *"The Bible (The Book of Exodus): Authorized King James Version,"* by Oxford University Press.

Siren (Σειρήν)/Sirenic: A creature in Greek mythology, often depicted as a woman with the lower body of a bird, who sings enchanting songs to lure sailors to their doom. Further reading: *"The Power of Myth,"* by Joseph Campbell and Bill Moyers.

Solomon/The Seal of Solomon (הַמֹּלְשׁ םָתֹח): A mystical symbol associated with *King Solomon,* a biblical figure known as the son of *King David* and *Bathsheba,* renowned for his wisdom, wealth, and the *First Temple in Jerusalem.* He is often depicted as a just ruler and a significant prophet in Jewish, Christian, and Islamic traditions. Solomon's *Seal* is often depicted cross-culturally as a hexagram or pentagram. In Jewish tradition, it is associated with Solomon's wisdom and divine power. Further reading: *"Picatrix: A Medieval Treatise on Astral Magic (Magic in History),"* by Dan Attrell and David Porreca.

Soma (सोम): A ritualistic drink in ancient *Vedic* tradition, believed to possess divine and mystical qualities. It was used in religious ceremonies and is mentioned extensively in the *Rigveda,* where it is associated with the gods *Indra* and *Agni. Soma* also symbolizes immortality and spiritual enlightenment. The exact nature and composition of the drink remain unclear. Further reading: *"Soma: Divine Mushroom of Immortality,"* by R. Gordon Wasson.

Sonder/Sondic: Refers to the realization that each person's life is as vivid and complex as one's own. The term is a neologism designed to evoke a particular emotional insight. Further reading: *"The Dictionary of Obscure Sorrows,"* by John Koenig.

Source: In spiritual contexts, *Source* denotes the divine or primary origin and cause of all existence. The ultimate reality. Further reading: *"The Perennial Philosophy,"* by Aldous Huxley; *"Tao Te Ching,"* by Lao Tzu, translated by Stephen Mitchell.

Sub-atomic: Refers to particles that are smaller than an atom, including *protons, neutrons, electrons,* and various other fundamental particles such as *quarks* and *gluons.* Further reading: *"The Elegant Universe: Superstrings, Hidden Dimensions, and the Quest for the Ultimate Theory,"* by Brian Greene.

T

Tao (道): *Tao* translates to "way," "path," or "principle" in English. It is a foundational concept within Chinese philosophy, particularly within *Taoism (Daoism)* representing the ultimate principle governing the universe, embodying the natural order of all things. In Taoist thought, the *Tao* is considered the source of existence and encourages living in harmony with the nature. Further reading: *"Tao Te Ching,"* by Lao Tzu, translated by Stephen Mitchell.

Tesla: *Tesla* is commonly recognized as the surname of *Nikola Tesla,* a Serbian-American inventor, engineer, and physicist, famous for his contributions to *alternating current (AC) electricity, wireless communication,* and other groundbreaking inventions. Further reading: *"My Inventions and Other Writings,"* by Nikola Tesla; *"The Inventions, Researches, and Writings of Nikola Tesla,"* by Nikola Tesla, edited by Thomas Commerford Martin.

Thou Shalt: An archaic phrase meaning "you shall" or "you must," used in the Bible's *Ten Commandments* to express moral or divine imperatives. It originates from Old English and Biblical Hebrew. Further reading: *"The Bible (The Book of Exodus): Authorized King James Version,"* by Oxford University Press.

Tiamat (✳ ⟁ ᵐ⧺): In *Mesopotamian* mythology, *Tiamat* is the primordial ocean goddess, symbolizing chaos and the untamed forces of nature. She is often depicted as a dragon or sea serpent, whose defeat by the god *Marduk* results in the creation of the world from her divided body, representing the battle between order and chaos. Further reading: *"Enuma Elish: The Babylonian Creation Epic,"* by Timothy J. Stephany; *"Myths from Mesopotamia: Creation, the Flood, Gilgamesh, and Others,"* translated by Stephanie Dalley.

Titans (Τιτάνες): In Greek mythology, *Titans* are the primordial deities who ruled during the *Golden Age,* preceding the *Olympian gods.* Known for their colossal stature and elemental powers, they were ultimately overthrown by *Zeus* and the *Olympians* in the *Titanomachy,* marking a significant shift in the divine hierarchy. Further reading: *"Theogony and Works and Days,"* by Hesiod, translated by M. L. West; *"The Greek Myths,"* by Robert Graves; *"Mythos: The Greek Myths Retold,"* by Stephen Fry.

Toska (Тоска): A Russian term for deep existential longing, sadness, melancholy, nostalgia, or spiritual anguish, often rooted in a yearning for meaning or connection. Further reading: *"The Complete Short Novels,"* by Anton Chekov, translated by Richard Pevear and Larissa Volokhonsky; *"The Brothers Karamazov,"* by Fyodor Dostoevsky, translated by Richard Pevear and Larissa Volokhonsky.

Tower of Babel (לְתֹּב לְדְגְמָ): A biblical narrative detailing humanity's hubristic attempt to construct a tower reaching the heavens, resulting in divine intervention causing the dispersion of people and the confusion of languages. Further reading: *"The Bible (The Book of Genesis): The Old Testament: Authorized King James Version,"* by Oxford University Press.

236

U

Upanishads (उपनिषद्): The *Upanishads* are ancient *Sanskrit* texts serve as the philosophical core of Hinduism. They are considered the concluding sections of the *Vedas,* specifically associated with *Vedanta,* meaning "the end of the Vedas." The *Upanishads* explore the relationship between the philosophical concepts found in the earlier portions of the Vedas, focusing on the nature of *Brahman* (the ultimate reality) and *Ātman* (the individual soul), emphasizing personal spiritual experience and meditation as paths to understanding existence. They mark a shift from ritualistic practices to philosophical inquiry in Hindu thought. Further reading: *"The Upanishads: A New Translation,"* by Eknath Easwaran.

.V

Vedanta (वेदान्त): *Vedanta* is a philosophical system derived from the concluding portions of the *Vedas,* particularly the *Upanishads,* and represents the culmination of *Vedic* thought. It focuses on the self's relationship to reality and offers various paths to spiritual liberation. It emphasizes ethical living and practical applications of philosophy. Further reading: *"A Thousand Teachings: The Upadeśasāhasrī of Śaṅkara,"* translated by Sengaku Mayeda.

Vedas (वेद): The ancient sacred Hindu Sanskrit scriptures: the *Rigveda, Samaveda, Yajurveda,* and *Atharvaveda.* They encompass a vast range of knowledge, including hymns, rituals, philosophy, and guidance for spiritual practice. Further reading: *"The Vedas: An Introduction to Hinduism's Sacred Texts,"* by Roshen Dalal; *"The Essential Vedanta: A New Source Book of Advaita Vedanta,"* by Eliot Deutsch and Rohit Dalvi.

Vesica Piscis: A geometric shape formed by the intersection of two circles, symbolizing the intersection of the spiritual and material worlds. Further reading: *"Sacred Geometry: Philosophy & Practice (Art and Imagination),"* by Robert Lawlor.

W

Wahdat al-Wujud (وحدة الوجود): Arabic for "Unity of Being," a concept in Islamic mysticism, particularly in *Sufism*, denoting the oneness of God and creation. It denotes the concept that there is no true existence other than the Ultimate Reality (God) and that all other forms of existence are manifestations of this single reality. Further reading: *"The Secrets of Secrets,"* by Hadrat Abd al-Qadir al-Jilani, translated by Shaykh Tosun Bayrak; *"Unity of Being: Islamic Mysticism and Sufism,"* by Seyyed Hossein Nasr.

Wajd (وجد): Arabic for "ecstatic love" or "spiritual rapture," often associated with *Sufi* practices, where one experiences a profound sense of connection with the divine. Further reading: *"Mystical Dimensions of Islam,"* by Annemarie Schimmel; *"The Translator of Desires: Poems,"* by Muhyiddin Ibn 'Arabi, translated by Michael Sells.

Wu wei (无为): Chinese for "non-action" or "effortless action," a *Taoist* principle of aligning with the universe's natural flow, embracing spontaneity, and allowing events to unfold naturally without undue interference or force. Further reading: *"Tao: The Watercourse Way,"* Alan Watts.

Y

Yahweh (יְהוָֹה): The Hebrew name for God. It is the divine name revealed to *Moses* in the *Hebrew Bible*, symbolizing God's eternal and unchanging nature, and serving as a key expression of monotheism in Jewish and Christian traditions. Further reading: *"The Bible: (The Old Testament) Authorized King James Version,"* by Oxford University Press.

Yantra (यंत्र): A mystical diagram used in Hinduism, Buddhism, and other Indian traditions, typically drawn or constructed geometrically, symbolizing the universe. *Yantras* are associated with deities and cosmic forces and are crucial in *tantric* practices as tools for meditation and worship. Further reading: *"Yantra: The Tantric Symbol of Cosmic Unity,"* by Madhu Khanna.

Z

Zen (禅): A Japanese school of *Mahayana Buddhism* emphasizing meditation and intuition over ritual worship and doctrinal study. *Zen* focuses on the direct experience of enlightenment *(satori)* through meditation *(zazen)* and mindfulness. Further reading: *"An Introduction to Zen Buddhism,"* by Daisetz Teitaro Suzuki; *"The Way of Zen,"* by Alan Watts.

Zephyr (Ζέφυρος): Derived from the Greek word "Ζέφυρος" (Zéphyros), god of the west wind, symbolizing a gentle breeze, seasonal changes, and renewal. Often depicted as a youthful figure, *Zephyr* is associated with the blossoming of flowers and the nurturing of crops, playing a crucial role in agricultural fertility and the life cycle. Further reading: *"The Iliad,"* by Homer, translated by Robert Fagles; *"The Gods of the Greeks,"* by Károly Kerényi.

www.ingramcontent.com/pod-product-compliance
Lightning Source LLC
Chambersburg PA
CBHW021227130626
46554CB00004B/1406